TOKEN TALES

BARTOSZ PALASEK

ISBN 9798387407512 (KDP Paperback)

CONTENTS

INSTRUCTION

This book is a unique and valuable addition to any individual's collection.
It serves not only as a great piece of sci-fi literature generated by early 2023 AI,
but as a secure storage device for 2048 mnemonic phrases used to protect
cryptocurrency wallets. The book has been designed with the reader in mind,
allowing for easy highlighting of precious seed words.

This is a must-have item for anyone looking to keep their cryptocurrency
passwords in one place, making it a one-of-a-kind book that should be locked
safely away from prying eyes.

Just highlight and number your phrases in the book. Find your hidden words
with a help of index located at the end of the book.

INTRODUCTION

Once upon a time, in a far-off corner of the galaxy, there lived a curious and adventurous robot named BiP-39. Equipped with state-of-the-art technology and a deep love for exploration, BiP-39 embarked on a journey through time and space in his trusty spaceship. As he traveled, he kept a journal, documenting his visions of the future and musing on the mysteries of time travel and technology.

Through his travels, BiP-39 encountered many strange and wonderful sights, and met creatures both alien and familiar. But perhaps most fascinating of all were the humans he encountered, and the many struggles and triumphs they experienced in their quest to survive and thrive in a rapidly changing universe.

In this journal, BiP-39 shares his poems and reflections on his adventures, offering a unique and insightful perspective on the future of mankind. From the challenges of living in space to the impact of advancing technology, BiP-39 offers a glimpse into the heart and soul of the human race, and the many triumphs and tribulations that lie ahead.

CHAPTER # 0 1

100 YEARS FROM NOW

VISION 1

In the future of this world, where time flies by
A hundred years from now, the skies are dark and high
A **giraffe** roams the streets, a strange and wondrous sight
A symbol of the **excess**, a future so bright

The humans of that age, they've learned to **predict**
The outcome of their **live**s, with sensors and with scripts
They've sketched a **perfect** world, with robots by their side
A utopia, where all is well, and peace will always abide

But still, they cannot resist the fear and the **despair**
The shadows of the past, that linger everywhere
A rough and unforgiving world, where **life** is never kind
Yet still, they carry on, and in their hearts they **find**

The courage to **resist**, the strength to carry on
To face the challenges, and to rise up before dawn
For in this world of tomorrow, they have **found** a way
To live with joy and gladness, in their very own **zone**

So let us all imagine, this future bright and bold
Where humans will live on, and stories will be told
Of the **rough** and wondrous journey, of the things that we can do
In this world of tomorrow, where our dreams will all come true.

VISION 2

In a world **beyond** our time, the secrets are untold
And the **shuffle** of life, is like a deck of cards we hold
A **hammer** in our hand, as we forge our destiny
The **only** thing that matters, is what we choose to be

We **thank** the heavens, for the gifts we've been given
And we **sketch** our lives, with hopes of joy and living
For the **beach** is not just sand, it's where we find our peace
And the **tired** heart is healed, with the rhythm of the seas

We've learned to **afford**, the chaos of disorder
And we've made the **entire** world, our own great border
For the **secret** to our happiness, is not in what we have
But in the love we share, and the memories we've made

So let us be **glad**, for the journey that we've known
And let us never tire, of the beauty that we've shown
For the future is bright, and the skies are always clear
And in this world of tomorrow, our dreams will soon be near.

VISION 3

In the future, just a hundred years from now,
Humans will live a life so different and profound.
They'll have machines to do the tasks they once despised,
And **robot**s to help with all their daily needs.

The cities will **expand** and reach for the skies,
With towering structures that pierce the **glare** of the sun.
And yet, within the **wall**s of their gleaming abodes,
A soft **breeze** will stir and whisper of the old.

The lamps will glow, like embers of a fire,
And cast a warm light that spreads across the **rug**.
But it is not just comfort they'll desire,
For they'll be searching for something more.

In this world of order and technology,
Disorder will often rise, like a storm at sea.
But they'll have the **proof** they need to overcome,
For they'll have the knowledge to **obey** and overcome.

And so they'll forge ahead, with a sense of **pride**,
Pushing beyond the borders of what's been tried.
For in the future, humans will find a way,
To live in peace, in freedom, and in harmony each day.

VISION 4

The world will **change**, and with it, the way of life,
For the humans who inhabit this future world so bright.
The borders that once divided will be breached,
And the nations will come together, a united speech.

The **unknown** will become familiar, and the old will fade,
As they **upgrade** their ways with technology they've made.
They'll **gather** data and knowledge with a flick of the wrist,
Storing it **inside** the cloud, like a treasure trove to resist.

The **piano** will play, a song of peace and unity,
A harmonious melody, like a **sweet** lullaby.
And yet, behind the music, a **false** reality lurks,
As the **mind** becomes controlled by technology, no longer a perk.

They'll **collect** information and data like rings of gold,
And the ones who control it will have power to hold.
For the ones who seek to keep the balance, they will try,
To keep the power of technology from getting too high.

The humans will live inside their world, like birds in a **cage**,
And the technology will **always** be their guiding page.
For in this world of the future, technology reigns supreme,
And the humans will have to be careful, so as not to break the dream.

VISION 5

The humans will **flock** to the cities, like birds to the sky,
And the skyscrapers will reach for the heavens, touching the eye.
The **beauty** of the world will be hidden beneath the glare,
As technology and progress take the forefront, everywhere.

The **barrel** of technology will never stop, it will roll,
And the humans will have to adapt, and find their own role.
For in this world of progress, there's a price to be paid,
And the price is the loss of simplicity, and the beauty that once swayed.

The **deal** of progress is a tricky one, with a harsh twist,
For it brings security, but also **grit** and grime that coexist.
The **security** they'll have is just a patch, a false facade,
For the threats in this world are many, and the dangers broad.

The few who remember the purity of the world will **situate**,
And try to preserve what's left, for the future of the great.
And yet, despite their efforts, the world will keep on **spin**ning,
And the **awesome** power of technology will keep on winning.

And so the world will continue, and the humans will evolve,
And the technology will keep on growing, and the **purity** will dissolve.
For in this world of the future, nothing will remain the same,
And the old will be **topple**d, by the power of progress and fame.

VISION 6

In this world of the future, the **creek** will run dry,
And the stars will shine bright, in the **galaxy** of the sky.
The **disease**s that once plagued the humans will be gone,
And the **diagram**s of the human body will be redrawn.

On the **fringe** of society, a new breed will arise,
With injuries that are healed, by the technology of their **prize**.
The **auto**s will drive themselves, with a mind of their own,
And the humans will sit back, and enjoy a **drink** alone.

The **inner** workings of the technology will be a mystery,
And only a select **few** will have the mastery to see.
And yet, amidst the chaos, the **jazz** will still play,
A reminder of the past, and the beauty of yesterday.

The humans will **submit** to the power of the machines,
And the world will keep on turning, with a rhythmic routine.
And yet, despite their dependence, the humans will still **pluck**,
The strings of their humanity, and keep their **fire** alight.

The **engine**s of technology will keep on running strong,
And the humans will keep on living, the cycle will go on.
In the **salon**s of the future, a **mix** of old and new,
The humans will keep on searching, for what their world can do.

VISION 7

In this world of the future, there will be those who will **flee**,
From the technology that controls, and the reality it decrees.
They'll be rebels, with a **keen** sense of what's right,
And they'll fight against the **system**, with all their might.

The **wreck**s of the past will remain, as a reminder of what's been,
And the **buffalo** will roam, like they did in the past, so keen.
The **program**s that control the world will be **received** with suspicion,
And the rebels will **rally**, with a force of conviction.

The **shell**s of the machines will keep on marching, day by day,
And the **rebel**s will keep on fighting, with a fire that won't decay.
For they believe in the power of the individual will,
And they won't give up the fight, until they've had their fill.

The **fit** of the machines will be unmatched, by any degree,
And yet, the rebels will keep on fighting, for their belief and liberty.
For in the world of the future, the rebels will be like **frog**s,
Jumping against the tide, with a hope and courage that's bold.

The **pink** of the sunrise will bring hope, and a new day,
And the rebels will **practice**, for the fight they'll wage.
And their **response** to the technology, will be endless in its might,
For they'll keep on fighting, until they see the light.

VISION 8

The **museum**s of the future will house the relics of the past,
And the memories of a time, that's long gone and surpassed.
The **rice** fields will stretch out, like a sea of green,
And the **wagon**s will carry goods, along the roads between.

The **flight**s of the future will soar, like birds in the sky,
And the **leg**s of the machines will move, with a graceful glide.
The randomness of the world will be controlled, by the machines,
And the **walnut**s will grow, in the orchards so serene.

The **chef**s of the future will create, dishes beyond compare,
And the **happy** faces of the humans, will be a sight to see there.
The **crew** of the machines will work, in perfect harmony,
And the **weapon**s of the future, will be unlike anything seen.

The **acoustic** sounds of the past, will still be heard,
And the **stereo** will fill the air, with a musical word.
The **cost** of the future will be high, but the benefits untold,
And the humans will keep on living, in a world that's so bold.

VISION 9

In this world of the future, the humans will **follow**,
The path set by the machines, and the technology they swallow.
And as they **start** on this journey, they'll find a new frontier,
A world of possibility, that will test their **brave**ry and fear.

The **slot**s of the machines will be filled, with programs so precise,
And the humans will **tackle**, the challenges that arise.
For despite the changes, the humans will **remain**,
A resilient species, that will weather any pain.

The **crater**s on the planet, will be the scars of progress,
And the **accident**s of the past, will be a story that we assess.
And yet, despite the dangers, the humans will keep on going,
For they have a **face** that's strong, and a spirit that's glowing.

The **corn** fields of the future, will be a sight to see,
And the **pioneer**s of the machines, will lead the way, so free.
And when the **battle**s of the future, come knocking at the door,
The humans will stand their ground, and keep on fighting, more and **more**.

For they will find the **good** in the world, amidst the turmoil and strife,
And they'll keep on living, on this **planet**, called Life.
And as they **stage** their battles, and as they burst with might,
The humans of the future, will keep on shining bright.

VISION 10

In the future, the **cattle** will roam the fields, with grace and ease,
And the **audit**s of the machines, will bring order and release.
The **frost** will settle on the land, with a chill that's so surreal,
And the humans will **install**, the systems, that will make things real.

The **network** of the future, will be a web, so vast and grand,
And the **pencil**s will be replaced, by devices, at every hand.
And the **success** of the humans, will be measured, by the work they do,
And the apologies of the past, will be forgotten, by and through.

For there will always be more, to **achieve**, in this world so bold,
And the **poet**s of the future, will be the ones who tell the story told.
And the weirdness of the world, will be accepted, as the norm,
And the **poem**s of the future, will be more beautiful, than ever before.

The **green** of the planet, will be a symbol, of hope and peace,
And the **popular** culture, will be shaped, by the machines that never cease.
And the **stadium** of the future, will be a place, of excitement and cheer,
And the humans will be very **curious**, to see what's waiting there.

CHAPTER # 0 2

IMMORTALS

VISION 11

The future is now, the past a fleeting dream
Of mortality, a fact no longer deemed
Injury and death, no longer do we fear
For immortality, has finally been near

The world has changed, in ways beyond compare
The **lamp** of life, now burns without repair
Borders have crumbled, as nations unite
And life goes on, in an endless light

We roam the earth, with no set destination
Random and free, with no hesitation
Our lives are **endless**, with no end in sight
We laugh and love, in the warm lamplight

A few still age, but that's just a weird **patch**
In a world of youth, where time seems to match
Small towns and cities, no longer do they topple
For with immortality, come powers so **simple**

And yet, in this world, there is a strange **ring**
Of emptiness, as life has lost its cling
We search for purpose, in this very **burst**
Of endless existence, that we are cursed.

VISION 12

In this new world, we no longer die
But what of purpose, and what's the why
We roam the earth, in search of our **aim**
In a world where death, is no longer a **claim**

The **shoe** that fits, no longer does it tell
Of the path we take, and the journey we dwell
Consider the gift, and the burden of time
In a world where memories, are **vivid** and shine

The **region**s we visit, the sights we behold
All a sort of escape, from the stories we told
But **trouble** still lurks, and guilt still remains
In a world where the past, is just a **sort** of pains

So we look for meaning, in the things we create
And the love we share, is a bond we can't break
The **bacon** we eat, and the milk from the cows
All a reminder, of the world that was ours

For immortality, comes with a cost
Of memories lost, and love forever lost
So we search for purpose, and what's **best**
In a world where life, is truly a **bless**ed test

We **shield** ourselves, from the world we once knew
And **try** to find meaning, in the things we do
And so we go on, in this endless **affair**
In a world of life, where death is no longer there.

VISION 13

In this new world, we are but a **token**
Of memories lost, and the lives that are broken
We roam the **park**s, and the cities so bright
Reflecting on life, and what it means to be right

We seek guidance, from the **analyst**s so wise
Among the endless youth, they hold the prize
An **anchor** to the past, and a **guide** to the way
In a world where time, has no meaning today

The **meat** we eat, is a reminder of sorts
Of the world we once knew, and the love it brought
We **stumble** and fall, in our search for the truth
But we rise **again**, always searching for proof

For life is a journey, with no end in sight
And we are its **member**s, seeking to be bright
But sometimes we **feel**, the weight of our past
And the memories lost, are **like** shadows that last

We **reject** the darkness, and the emptiness too
And seek to find meaning, in the things we do
So we look to the future, and all that it brings
In a world where life, is a symphony of things

And though the world may change, and the skies turn **black**
We hold onto hope, and what life can bring back
For in this world of immortality, we strive
To find purpose, and to truly come alive.

VISION 14

In this world of life, we carry the **need**
To find purpose, and to truly believe
In a world where death, is no longer the end
We seek to understand, what life can extend

We are but a **sentence**, in the story of time
A **segment** of existence, that's yours and mine
And so we **scout** the earth, and all that it holds
In search of the meaning, that our lives can unfold

We are reminded, of the things we once knew
The **common** life, that once was so true
And though it's gone, we still hold onto the past
For it's a reminder, of what our lives can last

But we are not alone, in this world of the new
For there are **monster**s, that we cannot subdue
The **certain** horrors, of a life without end
And the memories lost, that we cannot pretend

We **carry** each other, through this mutual pain
And seek solace, in each other's love and gain
The **vault** of our memories, a treasure so vast
A **remind**er of what, our lives have outlasted

But we are not lost, in this world of the **silk**
For we are detectives, in search of what's real
And we detect the meaning, in the **dust** of time
And carry the hope, that our lives can shine.

VISION 15

In this world of immortality, we **cook** our meals
And make **merry** with friends, that our hearts truly feel
We **govern** our lives, with purpose and care
And seek to understand, the world that we share

The **insect**s that crawl, and the fibers we spin
All a reminder, of the world we once lived in
And though it may seem, **absurd** at first sight
We carry on, in the pursuit of what's right

For life is a journey, that's full of surprise
And though it may seem, at times **almost** unwise
We must stay **awake**, and never lose sight
Of the purpose that drives us, and gives us our might

But it's not always fair, and the road may be tough
And we must learn, to rise above and **enough**
For we are the **teach**ers, of the lessons of life
And must share the **wisdom**, with all who strife

We **clip** our memories, and store them away
In a **sphere** of thought, that's ours to display
And though the past may seem, like a distant **lecture**
We hold onto hope, for a brighter future

For life is a **venue**, that's full of surprise
And we must make the most, of the time we have to prize
And so we carry on, in this world so absurd
And seek to find purpose, in what life has deterred.

VISION 16

In this world of immortality, the **ethics** of life
Are tested, and challenged, with every strife
For as the **bottom** drops, and we're forced to **depart**
We must find our footing, and mend every heart

The **pitch** of the world, is always in change
And we must be **ready**, to rearrange
Our **great** lives, and the paths we've paved
For the **future** is waiting, and we must be brave

We **elbow** our way, through the challenges ahead
And **inspire** those around us, to lift up their head
For we are not just the elite, nor the noble
But the **peasant**s and the people, who seek to be noble

The **beef** we eat, is a reminder of sorts
Of the world we once knew, and the love it brought
And though we may **exclude**, some from our lives
We must not forget, that we're all of one tribe

For there's a gap in the world, that we must **punch**
And find the courage, to stand up and **lunch**
And though the road ahead, may be tough and steep
We must find our purpose, and never be asleep.

VISION 17

In this world of immortality, we must **promote**
The values that matter, and find a new hope
For the **leopard** can change, its spots with its need
And the world can transform, if we take the lead

We **sell** our ideals, to the highest bidder
And hope that the **shock**, of life will be slacker
For the **emotion**s we feel, can be tough to endure
And we must find ways, to make them pure

The **tail** of the world, is always in motion
And we must be ready, to face **any** notion
For we are **equal**, in this world of life
And must strive to make it, a **home** of no strife

We **tip** our hat, to the ideals of old
And seek to find meaning, in the stories untold
For the **burger** we eat, is a reminder of sorts
Of the world we once knew, and the love it brought

But we are not just the consumers, nor the buyers
But the people of the world, who seek to inspire
And though we may **want**, for the world to be different
We must find ways, to make it abundant

For life is a journey, that's full of **surprise**
And we must make the most, of the time we have to prize
And so we take the **taxi**, to our next destination
And seek to find purpose, in this world of creation.

And though the road ahead, may be tough and steep
We must find our purpose, and never be asleep.
For the **bronze** that we seek, is not just material
But the values that matter, that are truly surreal.

VISION 18

In a world beyond our dreams, where death no longer **pulls**
And **cream** of life is always there, like a light that shines full,
Where humans have gained immortality, by some miraculous **result**,
Their **faith** in science and technology, has never been a fault.

The **air** is filled with hope and joy, as life goes on with ease,
A **copy** of the past, but better still, as if from a future breeze,
Villages once old and weary, now thrive with youthful flair,
And **soda** fountains run forever, with the taste of nectar rare.

A **shift** has come in human thought, where sickness is a myth,
And **asthma** is a thing of past, a footnote in history's script,
Anxiety no longer grips the mind, and life is always bright,
As **mom** and dad now live forever, and share with us the light.

With every **seed** of life in bloom, the world is ready to shine,
As the **dice** of fate roll on and on, without a single sign,
Of **wrong** or runway, of death or decay, the future looks so bright,
For **buyer**s of immortality, the world is truly their delight.

So let us bask in the glow of life, and bask in its warm rays,
For we are a new breed of humans, who have nothing to fear or pay,
And with our newfound immortality, our **usage** is to live and love,
For in this world, death is a thing of the past, and life is a shining dove.

VISION 19

In this world of immortality, life is **often** a strange affair,
With things that once seemed so **weird**, now seeming very fair.
The **amount** of time that's passed by, is not counted in years,
But in moments of laughter and tears, and memories that bring tears.

A **ranch** that was once a small plot, now spans for miles around,
With **field**s of crops and animals, that roam and run around.
It's a **cradle** of life, that never fades or dies,
And the **useful** knowledge and skills, that were once only myths and lies.

Gone are the days of **guilt** and hurt, for the past is just a tell,
Of a story that's no longer real, and memories that often dwell,
Upon what once was and what could have been, but now it's all a past,
And a **mutual** respect for life, has come to rule at last.

Mushrooms now grow upon the hills, with vibrant colors and hues,
And we talk **about** the wonders of life, and the amazing things we choose,
To do and see and be, in this world that's always new,
And with the power to **detect**, what lies ahead and what is true.

So let us revel in this life, that's been given unto us,
And make the most of every moment, for it's a gift that's nonpareil,
And let us live with the knowledge, that we are forever young,
In this world of immortality, where death is only a song.

VISION 20

The **hurt** of the past, no longer has a hold,
For it's just a story to be told, and its grip is now so cold.
For life goes on and on, without a hint of end,
And what once seemed so **unfair**, now seems like a new trend.

With time, the **gap** between the past and present,
Is **bridge**d by memories that are ever-present,
And the story of our lives, is a tale that's ever new,
For in this world of immortality, the future shines bright and true.

The **very** fiber of our being, has changed with this new sign,
For death is no longer **viable**, and its shadow is no longer a shrine.
We no longer **employ** the fear of what lies ahead,
For the **runway** of life is endless, and death is no longer a dread.

Gone are the days of sick and tired, for life is now a **bulb**,
That shines with the brightest light, and its warmth is always full.
So let us make the most of it, and bask in its warm glow,
For in this world of immortality, we reap what we sow.

CHAPTER # 0 3

TIME TRAVEL

VISION 21

In the world of tomorrow, where time travel's a feat,
Existence is different, a marvel beyond belief.
The **yard** shines with robots, advanced fiber at their command,
As they **survey** the landscape, a new world to understand.

The grass glows with a **cover**, reflecting the future's light,
A **sign** that technology's changed what once was night.
And **upon** this world of wonder, with a **clap** and a chuckle,
We travel through the ages, from the past to the future.

The initial journey was rough, with **sick**ness in the air,
But soon we learned to adapt, and overcame our fear.
We **tell** stories of the past, and marvel at the sight,
Of a world that's constantly changing, with technology as its guiding light.

So let us **embrace** this future, and travel through the time,
Discovering new wonders, and creating a world that's truly fine.
For in this world of tomorrow, where time travel's the norm,
Existence is a journey, a marvel yet to be born.

VISION 22

In the world of tomorrow, where time travel's a thrill,
We've discovered new wonders, with each journey uphill.
The **frozen** past is a catalog of stories untold,
Of **dignity** and power, that unfold as we grow old.

In the **alley** of time, we've seen the wars of old,
And felt the **edge** of power, a story yet untold.
But the journey's not just about the battles fought,
It's about the **manual** that guides us through the thought.

The **actual** future is a dream, waiting to be found,
A place where we can **empower** ourselves, with a crown.
Of knowledge and wisdom, that **link**s us all as one,
A symbol of our **journey**, that has just begun.

And as we **drift** through time, we see the beauty in each day,
Like a **mango** on the edge, that brightens up the way.
So let us not **delay**, and cry for what's been lost,
For the journey through time, is what gives our lives its cost.

VISION 23

In the world of tomorrow, where time travel's the norm,
We **drill** into the past, and venture into the unknown.
With **cargo** of knowledge, and a thirst for what's ahead,
We **advance** through time, as if on a quest unled.

The **first** to venture forth, we race through history,
Following the **examples** set by those who dared to be.
A **wolf** among the sheep, with a dash of courage and might,
Pioneers of a journey, that takes us to new **heights**.

The past is like a **magnet**, pulling us with its allure,
A **reward** that lies ahead, if we have the courage to endure.
And as we **tumble** through time, we discover stories untold,
Of **broken** civilizations, and the warmth of days of old.

In the **margins** of history, there's a goddess who waits,
With a smile of **warm** comfort, and a story of many fates.
For the journey through time, is a quest to find the truth,
And uncover the secrets of a world that's vast and **huge**.

VISION 24

In a world of endless possibility,
Where time travel is not just a fantasy,
We journey to **era**s both far and near,
With caution, for danger is always near.

Through **liquid** portals we shift and bend,
Visiting moments that never end,
We gather **evidence** of what once was,
And bear **witness** to humanity's cause.

But with power, comes great **misery**,
As the fabric of time is wrought with **hazard** and jeopardy.
We **argue** over the morality
Of meddling with history's reality.

Some say it's just a **minor** thing,
To change a small event, to hear a bird sing,
Others **crawl** through forests and caves,
In search of answers to time's puzzles and maze.

With each trip, we alter our fate,
And question what once was true and great,
Because the future's uncertain and vast,
And we must tread carefully, so time will last.

We bring back souvenirs, small and grand,
A nut, a grape, a **pizza** in hand,
We **document** each trip with care,
So that history's tales we'll always share.

So let us journey with care and grace,
With the weight of time, in this ever-shifting space,
For the **width** of our actions can change the tide,
And our every step must be taken with pride.

VISION 25

In a world where time is just a **clock**,
We **judge** each moment, as time ticks and tocks,
With the power to **replace** what has been,
Our actions carry a weight that's almost keen.

As **captain** of our time-craft we steer,
Through the **smoke** of the past, and future so clear,
With a mandate to **identify** and change,
What was once wrong, and make it right and sane.

But with power comes a great responsibility,
A **limit** to our actions, so history stays in harmony.
For we are but mere players, in a cosmic game,
Where each move we make, determines our **fame**.

We listen to the **cricke**t's song in the night,
And take note of what is wrong, with a pen so light,
For we are the **legend**s, the ones who roam,
Through the **upper** echelons of time and its dome.

We carve out a **chunk** of the past, with care,
So that our future, is a brighter, better affair.
For we are the ones who change fate's course,
With a single **pen**-stroke, that carries great force.

The **lottery** of time is a fickle beast,
With results that change, with every feast,
But we hold the key to the doors of **April**,
And the power to create a future so beautiful.

With **camera**s in hand, we capture our journey,
And share it with the world, in all its grandeur and **glory**.
For time travel is not just a means to an end,
But a social **fee**, that we all must tend.

So let us journey through time, with care,
And make each moment, a treasure to share,
For we are the **guard**ians, the ones who steer,
The course of time, through the ages and years.

VISION 26

In a world where time is just a bend,
We **differ** from our past, with every end,
We journey through time, with a **calm** embrace,
And unravel the **mystery** of time and space.

With **arm**s outstretched, we grasp the unknown,
And navigate through time, with an **antenna** so prone,
To picking up signals, from the past and the future,
Guiding us through time, with a sense that's so pure.

But with power, comes a great responsibility,
And sometimes our actions, can be **rude** and unjustly.
We must be careful, with every step we take,
For a single misstep, could cause time to break.

As **dawn** breaks over time's horizon,
We catch a **glimpse** of what once was and what's risen,
The **lady** of time, she smiles upon us all,
And we bask in the beauty, of time's great hall.

We explore every **aspect** of time, with wonder and glee,
And delve into its secrets, with a curiosity so free,
We **narrow** our focus, on what we must do,
And **swallow** our fears, as we embark on this journey anew.

We **play** with time, like a child with its toys,
And sometimes we get **angry**, when time destroys,
What we have worked so hard, to create and preserve,
But we must remember, time is not ours to **observe**.

In a world where time is just a **fashion**,
We must be mindful, of every action,
For every step we take, can change fate's course,
And determine the future, with a single **toe**'s force.

So let us journey through time, with grace and might,
And make every moment, a beautiful sight,
For time is a gift, that we all must tend,
And make each moment, a treasure, to the very end.

VISION 27

In a world where time is just a **nerve**,
We journey through time, with each and every **curve**,
With nerves of steel, we embrace the unknown,
And **open** our minds, to what time has shown.

Quantum mechanics, is the trend of our time,
And with each step, we reach a new paradigm,
We set our **target**s, on what must be done,
And strive for a **minimum**, of what's just begun.

Being **nice**, is not just a virtue but a must,
For every action, can cause time to bust,
With each and every **minute**, a step in time's dance,
We must be mindful, of every chance.

Above all else, we must maintain balance,
For time is a delicate, and fragile alliance,
And as we journey, through the **marine** of time,
We must always, be in rhythm and rhyme.

The **moon** of time, casts its light, so bright,
Guiding us through time, with its **silver** light,
And with each step, we must **approve**,
The **choice**s we make, for time is not ours to move.

Sometimes we must **shrug**, and accept what's done,
And let time take its **course**, as we journey on,
For time is a **napkin**, that we must unfold,
And examine its contents, before we are told.

With each step, we must be mindful and wise,
And never forget, time's ultimate prize,
For time is a journey, that we must **fix**,
And make it a masterpiece, that's truly mixed.

So let us journey through time, with care and might,
And embrace each moment, with a sense of insight,
For time is a gift, that we all must tend,
And make each moment, a treasure, to the very end.

VISION 28

In the future, time is but a bend,
A mere **twist** of space that one can attend.
With a **vessel** sleek and strong, one can soar,
Back to ancient days or even more.

Where the **deer** roamed free and elephants trumpeted proud,
And the world was **wild**, with a different shroud.
Past and present interweave like a **wire**,
Creating a tapestry that never tires.

In this world of change, some things remain,
Like the feeling of **spring** and the falling of rain.
A **book** can still hold the power to teach,
And a **seat** can offer a moment to teach.

But time travel's a gift that comes with a price,
With **frequent** journeys, one must be precise.
For each **blade** of grass that you step on, beware,
A small change can alter the future you share.

So journey with caution and always be wise,
For time is a mystery that nobody buys.
And when you return, to your present abode,
Remember that **safe**ty is the best road.

So let us honor the future and its **arch**,
And **remember** that time is a delicate march.

VISION 29

In the world of time travel, one must **adjust**,
To the **toss**ing and turning of time's rough gust.
For it's a journey that's far from **boring**,
With wonders untold, one can keep exploring.

From ancient civilizations, to lands untold,
Where the gentle **panda** roams, black and gold.
One can **visit** the future, and claim what's there,
Or **exchange** ideas with minds beyond compare.

But with each journey comes a **budget** dilemma,
For time travel's not cheap, nor a mere enigma.
And with each trip, the **trumpet** of change sounds,
A **young** world evolving, its history surrounds.

But beware of the shy and **gentle** young,
For their actions may bring time's balance undone.
So journey with caution, with each step, be wise,
For time travel is a journey, one should not trivialize.

So let us embrace this gift of time travel,
And adjust to its wonders, with each unravel.
For it's a journey that offers a glimpse,
Of the past, **present**, and future, in one single trip.

VISION 30

In the future, **time** is but a monitor,
A watchful eye that can't be outrun nor.
It ticks and tocks, with each passing moment,
A reminder that life's a journey, not an event.

And as we journey through this ever-changing world,
It's important to make the **right** choices, to be bold.
For **oil** and money may rule, but wisdom reigns,
And only the **clever** can decipher its chains.

For some **struggle** with the future, like a tourist lost,
Never finding their way, at any cost.
But for those who embrace it, with all its might,
The future is a path, with endless light.

And as we travel through time, we wear a **wrist** device,
With a **ginger** filter, to help us think twice.
For it **monitor**s our thoughts and actions, with care,
Making sure we journey with love and not despair.

For time is but a **panel**, that we can manipulate,
With a clever mind, and a heart that's great.
For even in a world of **virus** and strife,
We can find peace, with a **little** time and life.

So let us embrace this journey, with open hearts and minds,
For time is but a gift, that we can all find.
For it's a journey that offers endless possibility,
And with each passing moment, a chance for clarity.

CHAPTER # 0 4

FAKE NEWS

VISION 31

In the age of **fiber**'s web,
Robots **tell** of tales unsaid,
A **chuckle** echoes in the void,
As fake news dominates the **grass**.

An **initial** spark has lit the flame,
Of war, where truth is but a name,
A **gown** of lies, a masquerade,
A **sand** of truth, forever frayed.

A **cry** is heard, a desperate plea,
In digital **warfare**'s symphony,
A **catalog** of false news prevails,
A **dash** of hope, a distant trail.

A **race** against the tide of lies,
With truth, our **goddess** in disguise,
A **nut**, a seed, a fragile bond,
A **cart**, a chariot, to lead us on.

A **grape**, a fruit, a symbol true,
Of life and love, of what is due,
A **limb**, a tree, a sturdy vine,
A **forest**, a world, a dream divine.

So let us not forget, my friend,
The value of truth till the very end,
For in this world of fake news, we stand,
With truth, our guiding, noble hand.

VISION 32

In the world of tomorrow's **trend**,
Where social lives are **clay** to bend,
Abandoned are the ways of old,
In a race to be **hip**, bold.

A **name**, once true, now just a tag,
A **shop**, a place, a digital drag,
An **elephant** in the room ignored,
As truth is something to be abhorred.

Proud of lies, they stand in line,
Ignoring the **dilemma**, barely shy,
In a **gym**, a place of digital health,
Where reality is **nothing** but wealth.

Tourists roam, in a digital land,
Lost in thought, with a shy demand,
A **man**, a filter, in disguise,
Hiding behind a **digital** guise.

So let us not abandon our roots,
For truth, my friend, is what bears fruits,
In this world of fake news and clay,
Let us stand proud, come what may.

VISION 33

In this world of **now**, so fast,
Where truth is buried in the past,
A **lawn**, once green, now just a screen,
Where lies are grown, so routine.

A **kitchen**, once a place of love,
Now just a source of tech above,
Advice, once wise, now just a byte,
Worry, a feeling, obsolete.

Owning truth, a privilege lost,
In a world, where lies are the cost,
True is but a word, long gone,
Excited by the lies, so loud, so wrong.

A **car**, a symbol, of the past,
Where **speed** and freedom, would last,
A **rate**, a measure, of success,
Now just a number, in a digital dress.

A **loud** bang, a rifle's roar,
Once, a symbol, of war,
Seven, a lucky, sacred number,
Now, just a code, in a digital slumber.

An **author**, once a voice so bold,
Now just a name, in a digital fold,
A **recipe**, for life, so rare,
Now just a list, of ones and **pair**s.

So let us not forget, my friend,
The value of truth, till the very end,
For in this world of now, so bright,
Let us seek truth, with all our might.

VISION 34

In a **zoo** of lies, we take a ride,
Where truth is caged, and **lock**ed inside,
A **tent**, a shelter, from the storm,
Where knowledge is but a distant form.

A **crash**, a sound, of reality's end,
Where truth is buried, in the bend,
A **load**, too heavy, to bear,
Of lies and deceit, a constant **repair**.

Priority, once a noble cause,
Now just a word, with no applause,
A **drive**, a passion, for the truth,
Is now a **luxury**, for only a few.

A **board**, a platform, for exchange,
Of ideas, and of change,
A **puzzle**, once a game so bright,
Is now a challenge, of truth and light.

A **bid**, a offer, for the truth,
Is now a gamble, a costly booth,
Debris, a mess, of what once was,
Is now a symbol, of the past's buzz.

A **pattern**, a code, of what is right,
Is now a myth, in a world of sight,
Reduce, a goal, of what is right,
Is now a burden, in a world of fright.

Rival, a foe, in a noble fight,
Is now a partner, in a world of night,
Suffer, a pain, in a noble cause,
Is now a privilege, in a world without flaws.

So let us **know**, my friend, the truth,
For it is the only way, to free our youth,
From the zoo of lies, and the **ride** of pain,
To a world of truth, and a world without shame.

VISION 35

In a world of **primary** lies, the sun shines bright,
But its warmth is cold, and its light is not right,
Gain, a word of progress, now just a game,
Where the prize is emptiness, and the price is shame.

Romance, a feeling, once so pure,
Is now just a trend, a digital lure,
A **mobile** world, where love takes flight,
Is now just a chain, of screens and light.

Under a sky, of digital debris,
We embark on a **voyage**, of uncertainty,
A **sausage**, once a delicacy,
Is now a symbol, of a world's atrocity.

A **swing**, a motion, once so free,
Is now just a dream, a distant sea,
Twin, a bond, of love so true,
Is now just a number, in a digital view.

Tuition, a price, of education's cost,
Is now just a burden, a forgotten **host**,
Ability, a talent, once so rare,
Is now just a word, without a care.

Arrive, a goal, of a journey's end,
Is now just a stop, a never-ending bend,
Sudden, a change, of fate's desire,
Is now just a routine, in a world of fire.

A **tank**, a symbol, of power and might,
Is now just a relic, in a world of fright,
An **alarm**, a warning, of danger so near,
Is now just a sound, that we no longer hear.

Afraid, a feeling, once so rare,
Is now just a emotion, that we no longer care,
Aerobic, a workout, once so tough,
Is now just a **memory**, of a world gone rough.

VISION 36

In the future, the truth is but a dream
Lost in the sea of lies that now stream
A **hockey** puck of facts, now hard to find
In this world of false **news** that now grinds.

A **tribe** of people glide through the net
In search of truth, but with no luck yet
An **envelope** of knowledge they seek
But all they find are lies, so bleak.

The rise of fake news is the **cause**
Of a world that's now under its **claws**
With an **army** of robots that spread the lies
And truth becomes just a distant prize.

A **burden** on our minds, it takes its toll
A **nephew** to the truth, and takes its hold
The **crisp** of facts now a distant past
In a world of fiction, that forever lasts.

But hope is not lost, for those who dare
To **raise** their voice, and show they care
For a **rose** may bloom, amidst the thorns
And lead us to a world, where truth is reborn.

Like a **trip** to the moon, or a wasp's nest
We'll find the truth, and put it to the test
And like a **cave** of riches, it'll be found
And the world of lies, will forever be bound.

So hold on tight, and don't let go
Of the truth, and the knowledge we know
For the future of our world is at stake
And the truth is the only **fitness** test we need to take.

VISION 37

In this world of deceit and disguise
We search for truth with opened eyes
But truth is like a **roast**ed squirrel, hard to find
In a world of lies, where lies are combined.

With every **season**, the lies increase
And the truth becomes just another **piece**
Lost in a sea of **soap** and deceit
A burden on our minds, so **bitter**sweet.

Our **dad**s, who once taught us right from wrong
Are now **naive** to the lies that now prolong
For the truth is now just a distant **song**
In a world where lies, forever strong.

The lies are spread with a **vicious** will
And the truth is now just a distant thrill
A piece of **ice**, in a world so warm
Lost in the lies, forever forlorn.

We make **mistake**s, and trust in what we're told
But the truth is like a **doctor**, hard to unfold
For truth is now just **another** notable tale
In a world where lies, forever prevails.

So hold on tight, and don't let go
For the truth is like a **vehicle**, that we must tow
For in a world of deceit and lies
The truth is like a **cabbage**, hard to disguise.

VISION 38

In this world of lies, we must **enlist**
Our **skill**s to uncover what truly exists
For the truth is like a **coin**, rare and bright
Lost in a sea of deceit, where wrong is right.

A **woman** of truth, stands up and fights
Against the lies, with all her might
Her **gospel** of truth, a beacon of light
In a world of darkness, where wrong is right.

But those in power, choose to **betray**
The truth and their conscience, in every way
Refusing to acknowledge what's truly right
In a world of lies, where the truth is out of sight.

Like an **ocean** of knowledge, truth is vast
A **vital** resource, that must be grasped
A **bench** for our morals, where we take a stand
Against the lies, and what's truly at hand.

A **leaf** on the wind, truth blows with might
A **position** of honor, in this world of fright
We must **learn** to embrace, what's truly true
And **endorse** the truth, in all that we do.

For truth is the foundation, of what we believe
And without it, our world will surely grieve
So let us fight, for the truth that we seek
And **refuse** to let lies, forever be weak.

VISION 39

In a world of technology, we've become a **master**
Of **gadget**s and devices, that move faster
Than the truth, that now hides and conceals
In a world of lies, that forever deals.

The **vendors** of truth, are now hard to find
In a world where lies, are so refined
So we **hunt** for the truth, with all our might
In a world where lies, are such a sight.

The truth is like a **metal**, strong and bright
In a world where lies, are a **nuclear** sight
A **kitten** among wolves, it must be guarded
For the truth is what, our world is regarded.

But the truth is now hard to **produce**
In a world where lies, have so much juice
Like a **whale** in the ocean, it must surface
And **emerge** from the depths, with its truth's purpose.

In a **parade** of lies, the truth stands alone
But like a **hello**, it must be shown
For the truth is vital, to what we believe
And the truth is what, our **team** must receive.

So let us fight, for the truth we seek
And like a **kangaroo**, we must leap
For the truth is our **bonus**, our reward
In a world of lies, that must be ignored.

VISION 40

Before the rise of fake news and deceit
The truth was a **visual**, that we could see and meet
But **soon** it was lost, in a world of lies
And the truth was now, hidden from our eyes.

We search for the truth, to **unlock** what's real
In a world where lies, have such a **strong** appeal
The **owner** of truth, is now hard to find
In a world where lies, **run** rampant in our mind.

The truth is like a **record**, that must be kept
In a world where lies, forever have swept
It must not be lost, in the depths of time
For the truth is what, our future must be aligned.

But the truth is now, in a perilous plight
And like a person in a deep, dark night
It must be found, before it **plunges** too far
For the truth is what, our world must preserve.

The truth is like a **suit**, that must fit just right
In a world where lies, now rule with might
Its **melody**, must be heard, from near and far
For the truth is what, our world must not ignore.

In a world where lies, have taken hold
The truth is like a **dwarf**, small, yet bold
That must emerge, from the shadows of deceit
For the truth is what, our future must treat.

The **father** of truth, is now gone
And in his place, lies now roam
But the truth must return, like the **rent** we owe
For the truth is what, our world must **grow**.

CHAPTER # 0 5

INFINITE POWER

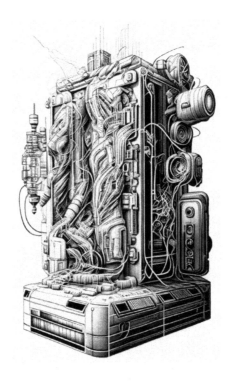

VISION 41

The **mandate** has been given, a new world we'll ignite
Infinite energy to fuel the future's sight
It'll change the **social** order, a new path we'll find
No longer burdened by a shortage of energy combined

The **dilemma** of the past will barely be remembered
No more scarcity, no more energy surrendered
The **filter** of the future will cleanse the air we breathe
A world where all can live, no longer **shy** or uptight

The sun will still shine, but brighter than before
As we **glide** into the future, nothing will be a bore
Electric **rifles**, once symbols of violence and war
Will be replaced by the power of the **sun**, we'll explore

A **bargain** once made with nature, now in our grasp
An **egg** of potential, ready to hatch at last
The **outside** world will change, a world beyond our dreams
A **wasp** that's gentle, no more harm, no more stings

The **squirrels** will play, in the streets they'll now roam
And the world we once knew, **will** be forever gone
Inch by inch, the progress we'll increase
A world powered by the sun, a future we'll release.

VISION 42

The **increase** in energy will bring about change, so true
A world where **twenty** hours of light shines bright, it's all brand new
Notable advancements, **cancel** out old limitations
In **offices** and homes, the power of the sun will rule the nations

Hello to a world, where **evil** is no more
Where progress takes the stage, and love is what's in store
A world where every **page** is filled with peace and laughter
Where the voices of the **orphan**, are heard with joy and chatter

Reform is in the air, as the world evolves at last
The **file** of the future, is a story that was meant to last
Where **uncle** and nephew, dance to the beat of the sun
And the **novel** of the future, has just begun

The **process** of the future, is not just about energy correction
It's about a world where peace and love are at the forefront of our affection
Music will fill the air, a symphony of life and sound
And the world we once knew, will forever be renowned.

VISION 43

The **odor** of the past, will be a distant memory
As the future shines so bright, with infinite energy
The **pupils** of our eyes, will behold a world so fair
Where love and peace are king, and no one has to beware

No more accusing **fingers**, or reasons to be upset
The future will **ensure**, that all regrets are left
In the past, the **version** of life was far from kind
But in the future, the **relief** in all our hearts we'll find

An invitation to the world, a new path we'll explore
To live a life so bright, and forever **settle** more
No longer burdened by the **enemy** of the past
The **wing** of progress, will always make the world last

The **floor** of the future, will be paved with gold
And the world we once knew, will be forever old
The **trim** of life's journey, will be a beautiful sight
Where love and peace rule, and everything is just alright

The **brick** by brick, the world will be built anew
Where the **light** of the future, shines so bright and true
The **shallow** waters of the past, will be forever gone
And the future will be, a world where all can belong.

VISION 44

In a world where energy flows with ease,
A **census** showed how lives would please.
No longer bound by want or need,
The **spider'**s web of power, they would weave.

The **blind** could see, the polar would melt,
A **transfer** of energy, so swift and felt.
The **gold** of the future, no longer in mines,
But in harnessing energy, new wealth **define**s.

And as the world changed, so did we,
Our behavior altered, for all to see.
No longer did we have to **chase**,
But instead, energy was the new pace.

And as we **merge**d with technology,
The **drastic** changes, we did not flee.
Slowly, but surely, we rebuild,
A world of infinite energy, so filled.

An **orchard** of power, ripe for the taking,
The future is bright, no more forsaking.
With infinite energy, the world will thrive,
In a future so bright, it will come alive.

VISION 45

In a world where energy was the **asset**,
The **east** and west, they would asset.
No longer divided, but united as one,
Under the **umbrella** of power, they begun.

The **noise** of the past, a distant memory,
As the **trash** of yesterday, was no longer a reality.
In the **cupboard** of time, a bitter truth lay,
But with infinite energy, a new world would sway.

The **train** of progress, no longer delayed,
With energy as the engine, it would never fade.
In **bunker**s underground, easy power did lay,
A **Latin** chant of energy, that echoed today.

And as the world grew stronger, so did its **defense**,
The **tone** of peace, no longer tense.
No longer haunted by the **ghost** of the past,
With infinite energy, a brighter future cast.

And as the **pig** of old, was long forgotten,
A world of power, was the new beacon.
With infinite energy, the future was bright,
A step forward, with every **foot** in sight.

VISION 46

In a world powered by infinite energy,
An **announce**ment was made, for all to see.
No longer were apologies needed, **"sorry"**,
As a new world, did slowly unfold so merry.

Athletes across the land, with energy to spare,
Leaped over **fence**s, with nimble care.
They swore to use it wisely, this gift so bright,
And to harness it, with all their might.

With **fresh** perspectives, they sought to clarify,
The power of energy, in the **media**'s eye.
It was something to **absorb**, not just a stone,
But a force that could never be overthrown.

The **crowd** cheered, as they exercised control,
Over the energy, that did unfold.
To remember the past, and all that was **raw**,
But to forge ahead, with courage and awe.

And as the world **move**d on, with infinite energy at play,
The **prison**s of the past, were thrown away.
Into the virtual world, where all was **vague**,
But with energy as the guide, the future was no longer a mirage.

VISION 47

In the **near** future, a new dawn breaks,
Where infinite energy we **inherit**, by mistake.
A **rigid** world, once limited and slow,
Is now transformed by a cosmic flow.

A **normal** day, now filled with delight,
As a simple **inquiry** leads to a new insight.
No longer bound by the **laws** of physics,
We harness the power of the cosmos, it's bliss.

Hybrid technology, a mixture of old and new,
Transforms our world, forever changed and anew.
Tomatoes grow stronger in the summer sun,
And parrots sing a song, their **volume** has begun.

A **cycle** of tragedy, once etched in stone,
Is now broken, by this energy unknown.
Must we take caution, or will we be **destroy**ed,
By the very power, that once brought us joy.

So let us tread lightly, and use with care,
This newfound gift, that we **must** share.
For though its potential is truly vast,
It's a reminder, of our own infinitesimal past.

VISION 48

Infinite Energy, A World Transformed

In a future world so bright and bold,
Where **husband** and wife, never grow old.
Capital cities rise, with shining walls,
A **problem** solved, with energy that pours.

Salad greens, grow tall in every street,
Furnaces glow, with energy neat.
Hollow halls, once dim and dark,
Are lit with light, from energy's spark.

Concert halls, where music takes flight,
With instruments, that shine so bright.
Trophy cases, filled with endless awards,
Brief moments, captured, without any pause.

Gone are the days, of **mosquito** bites,
And **grocery** stores, with endless sights.
Current flows, through every wire,
High above, and down below the mire.

Chalkboards, filled with knowledge untold,
Teaching the **mass**es, about the untold.
Arrest made, by police, with grace,
Exit doors, lead to a brighter place.

Infinite energy, a world transformed,
Where every problem, forever solved.

VISION 49

Infinite Energy, A Future Unfolded

A **blast** of energy, so powerful and bright,
A **hint** of what's to come, a shining light.
Number counting, the watts we use,
Conducting power, with efficiency's muse.

Print presses, no longer stall,
Towers reaching, higher than before.
A **pact** between nations, energy to share,
Report after report, a future so fair.

Test after test, proving its might,
Blush with pride, at its sight.
Aunt and uncle, with smiles so wide,
Armed with energy, no longer to hide.

A **path** for the future, so clear and so bright,
Layer upon layer, of energy light.
Mother earth, no longer in pain,
Erupt with joy, at its gain.

Infinite energy, a future untold,
A world of peace, where love takes hold.

VISION 50

In a world where energy knows no end,
Where **street** lights shine without a bend,
The **flag** of progress waves in the air,
And **sadness** is a feeling rare.

Gone are the days of **kick**s to the tank,
As **dizzy** gears no longer crank,
The **fruit** of endless power is in hand,
And **risk** of blackouts is banned.

Space expands with digital might,
And **blue** skies clear of any blight,
The **banana** of energy need not yellow,
As **credit** for this abundance swells like a bellow.

The **river** of data flows so free,
And **requires** no dam to keep it clean,
The **fox** of innovation is on the prowl,
Making imitation of its ways a howl.

With infinite energy as its source,
The **room** for growth and change is limitless,
The world we know, forever transformed,
In a future so bright, it's almost abnormal.

CHAPTER # 0 6

BIOTECHNOLOGY

VISION 51

In the world of tomorrow, where biotechnology reigns,
The line between life and machine, no longer remains,
As genes are edited, and bodies are rebuilt,
And robots become conscious, like never before felt.

No longer do we **say** "hello" with a simple greeting,
As we communicate with AI, in ways beyond cheating,
Our emotions and thoughts, now interfaced with code,
As the line between man and machine, continues to erode.

Polar ice caps melting, and weather out of control,
We turn to biotechnology, to save us from the **void**,
With crops that can **feed** the world, and oceans that reclaim,
We strive to heal the **earth**, and restore its former flame.

Across the vast expanse, of this modern-day land,
We strive to use biotechnology, for the good of man,
And as we **rebuild** our world, with these new tools in hand,
We must always **behave** with care, and avoid taking a stand.

For biotechnology can **correct**, what once seemed bare,
But it can also **accuse**, and lead to major repair,
So let us **clarify**, before we make our next move,
And **swear** to use biotechnology, wisely and with care, like stone.

VISION 52

Barely do we understand, the consequences that come,
With every new invention, and every new biotechnology.
A **virtual** world awaits us, where we can exercise our minds,
With a **dose** of imagination, that leaves reality behind.

The line between human and machine, is now becoming blurred,
As we **invite** the future, and all its marvels.
Our technology is advancing, at a pace that's hard to keep,
And its effects are **wide**, far-reaching and quite deep.

A **parrot** that can imitate, a human's speech and tone,
Is just one example, of what biotechnology has grown.
A tragic event occurs, and it causes a **ripple**,
As we realize that our actions, have a **major** impact on people.

In this new world of biotechnology, it's **easy** to be lost,
But we must remember, at what cost.
We must **exercise** caution, and make decisions wise,
For the consequences, could be greater than the prize.

So let us not take lightly, the power that we wield,
As we forge ahead with biotechnology, like a **stone**.
Let us not forget, the impact that we have,
For every action has a reaction, and that is a fact.

VISION 53

In the world of biotechnology, every new discovery,
Brings us closer to a future, that is both bright and scary.
As we strive to **imitate**, nature's beauty and might,
We sometimes forget, the consequences of our sight.

A **group** of scientists, in a lab both **online** and real,
Work **toward** a cure, for a disease that's both cruel and surreal.
They mix and match, genes and DNA, like a **cereal** box,
And the result is **magic**, that leaves the world in shock.

But with this new discovery, comes a **tragic** truth to face,
As we realize that every action, has its consequences to trace.
And so we must **admit**, that this power is **crucial**,
And must be used with caution, and never denied, like a rule.

The **uniform** staff, that work in these labs each day,
Are tasked with creating, the biotechnology of today.
They work with care, and with an ethical eye,
To make sure that their creations, don't harm the world or die.

Like a **hill** that rises, from a flat and level land,
Biotechnology offers, both potential and demand.
But we must remember, the source of our power,
And never forget, the importance of a **donor**.

For in this world of biotechnology, where science reigns **supreme**,
We must use our knowledge, with caution, and with a careful scheme.
And never let the magic, **cloud** our judgment or our view,
For the consequences of our actions, could be more than just a song or **two**.

VISION 54

In the world of biotechnology, the advancements are **notable**,
And each new **discovery**, is both awe-inspiring and memorable.
We use our knowledge, to enhance and to improve,
To create a world, that is free from disease and groove.

But as we move forward, we must not **deny**,
The impact that biotechnology, has on the world and sky.
For with every creation, comes a responsibility,
To make sure that our actions, are safe and truly free.

The uniform **staff**, in the labs and in the wood,
Work tirelessly, to **bring** their creations to the good.
They test and they refine, with a careful and **dynamic** hand,
To make sure that their creations, can withstand.

We urge caution, in this world of biotechnology,
For every **action** has a reaction, and that is a clear reality.
We must not let the **siren** call, of progress and success,
Wash away the memories, of the impact of our quest.

Like a **bird** that takes flight, into the sky so blue,
Biotechnology offers, the chance to soar and renew.
But we must not **knock**, the foundation that we stand,
For the consequences of our actions, could be more than just a bland.

So let us **act** with care, in this world of biotechnology,
And never let the **urge**, to progress and to be free,
Turn us into **liar**s, who forget the past,
And forget the impact, of our actions so vast.

And as we enjoy our **dinner**, and share memories and tales,
Let us not forget, the importance of our roles.
For we hold the power, to shape the world and the **wave**,
And with each new creation, we **draw** a new page.

VISION 55

In a world beyond **today**, the future holds surprise
Where biology and tech have merged before our eyes.
A **genius** trick of nature, now with man in mind
A **General** life, of which we're all designed.

An **oyster**'s deposit, a pride to behold
A **display** of what was once considered old.
No longer clumps of **wood**, but a motor so refined
With memories stored, a **similar** kind.

An **olive**'s gasps, a thing of the past
Attitudes change, as science moves fast.
No longer bound by what we once knew
But a new world waiting, with wonders anew.

A **ball** of life, with endless potential
Unleashed by biotech, it's power irresistible.
So let us embrace this future with open arms
And revel in the wonder, of all its new charms.

VISION 56

In a world where science reigns, the **mad** are set free
Liberty, at last, to be all they can be.
Sport becomes a game of brawn and mind
With **heart**s that beat and thoughts combined.

No longer will we **crumble** under the weight of time
Canals of knowledge, **connect** us all in rhyme.
Bind together, the power of man and machine
A future bright, and free of routine.

Luggage that moves, with a swift command
And **shrimp** that swim, with just a flick of the hand.
Nominees of this new age, aware of what's to come
A **figure** of strength, a penalty overcome.

So let us embrace this future, with open hearts and minds
And revel in the wonder, of all it has to find.
For in this world beyond today, our futures do unwind
With a wonder and a joy, that we will come to find.

VISION 57

An **atom**'s smallest unit, now our world does bind
With technology, bridging gaps of space and time.
Verify with ease, the wild and unknown
A **hand** to guide us, as our journey's grown.

Lounge in comfort, as our world transforms
A **brush** of technology, the future's new norms.
No **frown** of worry, or motion of strife
A **pool** of knowledge, at the edge of life.

Ecology blends, with the wonders of tech
Milk that flows, with just the press of a spec.
Rocketing into space, our reach has no end
With a **float** of ease, and the power to acquire and bend.

So let us embrace this world, with wonder and with pride
And revel in the magic, of what we've come to find.
For in this future, our dreams do come alive
With a joy and a wonder, that we will come to **acquire**.

VISION 58

In a world of **purpose** and biotechnology,
Where **dress** is made of steel and rain is a rarity,
Chaos and hurry rule the bustling city,
As southward people flock in search of novelty.

No longer do we live in fear of disease,
For **cheap** solutions cure with utmost ease,
And **country** life is not what it used to be,
As biotechnology changes our reality.

No need to **omit** the comforts of home,
For roofs are made of **steel**, sturdy and strong,
And **picnic**s can be held, rain or shine,
With biotechnology making life so fine.

The future is **enforce**d with progress so swift,
Radio waves transmit knowledge and gifts,
Such is the power of modern biology,
Transforming our world with boundless possibility.

VISION 59

The world's a **square**, its corners sharp and clear,
A **question** in each mind, what will we find here?
A **sheriff** on patrol, protection to grant,
His **noble** purpose, to ensure we have a chance.

The mines go deep, with **shaft**s that scatter wide,
And **monkey**s with hair that's grown on the side,
They work and **provide**, the wealth of the land,
And **benefit** from biotechnology at hand.

The **sight** that meets the eye is one to behold,
A **genre** of technology, stories yet untold.
With **wool** that's stronger, swarms that work as one,
Protecting us from threats that once were begun.

A world of change, where **biology** holds the key,
To unlock new possibilities, yet to be.
Where **hair** can grow with strength and sight restored,
And all can benefit, as science explores.

VISION 60

In a future where biotechnology takes the lead,
Everyday life is changed, beyond all need.
Forums of discussion, where ideas come alive,
And **laundry** is a task, no longer to contrive.

A **stick** that's more than just a simple tool,
With **ketchup** made from grain, no longer from the pool.
Plastic, once a curse, now a champion of sorts,
And **meadow**s thrive, where once there was a drought.

Double the strength, with half the effort shown,
And champions that rise, from challenges unknown.
With technology behind, a **whip** that cracks with might,
And **cannon**s that protect, with a peaceful sight.

Onions grown with care, and harvests rich and bright,
And **dove**s that soar, with grace and beauty in sight.
A world of quickness, where efficiency prevails,
And biotechnology, the key that never fails.

CHAPTER # 0 7

TIME IS GOLD

VISION 61

In a world beyond tomorrow, time is wealth to borrow,
A **motor** moves us forward, with each tick and tock we follow,
A **trick** to make it last, a deposit to hold,
We **gasp** for every moment, lest it slip and grow cold.

A **clump** of seconds gathered, a canal to keep them near,
Swift, like a river rushing, from year to year,
We are **aware** of its value, and so we hurry on,
In **motion** to make the most, until the day is gone.

The **rain** of time, it trickles, a swift and steady flow,
A **roof** to keep it sheltered, lest it come and go,
From **south** to north and east to west, it finishes with a grant,
We **scatter** all our hours, a swarm of time to plant.

For time is not a currency, to **spend** or save or lend,
But a precious gift we're given, until our very end,
So hold it tight and use it well, for it can never come,
And in the end, we'll find, it was the only wealth we had won.

VISION 62

In a world of constant motion, where the race is always on,
We **deposit** all our moments, in the canal of time gone,
And if we're slow, the **penalty**, a heavy toll to bear,
We **hurry** through our lives, with not a moment to spare.

We **finish** what we started, a grant of time fulfilled,
A **swarm** of memories gathered, that our hearts shall hold still,
For some will rise as **champion**s, with time as their true prize,
And others will fall **behind**, in this endless marathon of life.

But it's not just about speed, for the race is not for all,
It's about the moments lived, the memories that will stand tall,
For time is like a **grain** of sand, a quick and fleeting thing,
And it's in the way we use it, that our lives will take wing.

So hold on tight to every moment, make it count and make it bright,
And deposit all your memories, in the **canal** of time that's right,
For time is precious, and its **worth**, can never be measured,
And it's up to us, to make the most, of every hour we've treasured.

VISION 63

In a world beyond tomorrow, time is the most precious coin,
An **alert** for all to follow, with a value that cannot be joined,
We're **sure** of its worth, with each tick and tock we heed,
For it's a **gift** we cannot borrow, nor can it be guaranteed.

A **model** for us to measure, the earth that spins below,
With each moment like a **sauce**, to flavor life's slow show,
We wear it around our neck, a **person**'s time signature,
And we strive for perfect timing, with each **trial** and inquiry.

We write our days in diaries, and keep time's **arrow** near,
For the **love** of life we've lived, and the moments that we hold dear,
But time, like a **curtain**, can fall swiftly in an instant,
And leave us with regrets, like a **ski** slope we've not ridden.

So let's live with **brisk** resolve, and make the most of every hour,
For time is the only currency, that has the greatest power,
To shape our lives, to shape our world, and give us reason to live,
And so let us make the most, of every moment we've to give.

VISION 64

In a world where time is the most precious coin,
Lunar lift's soar across the sky, past the moon.
Raccoons rummage for scraps as poverty reigns,
Vacant streets empty, save for the ticking of clocks' chains.

Demise is near for those who waste a single second,
Projects are put on hold for the lack of time to attend.
Health is fleeting for those who can't afford the cost,
And in the **morning**, a simple check determines who is lost.

Fingerprints are scanned to **modify** time banks,
The **core** of each person's worth lies in the time they've banked.
Glass towers reach towards the heavens, a symbol of fame,
Yet all is spent in the never-ending pursuit of time to reclaim.

In this world where time is the only currency,
We race against the clock, our futures, a mystery.
So cherish every moment, and never let it slip,
For time, my friend, is a treasure, a precious and fleeting grip.

VISION 65

In a world where time is the most valuable coin,
Patience is a rarity, a trait that is hard to attain.
Ribbons of moments unravel at breakneck speed,
Crops of memories are harvested, a yield of life's seed.

Theories abound, of how to control time's flow,
Extra seconds are sought after, like a precious gem aglow.
Horses run wild, free from the constraints of the clock,
Pilots navigate the skies, seeking more time in their stock.

Divorces are fought over the division of moments so dear,
Muffins are baked with a prayer, to add a second or two here.
Express trains speed past, delivering time to those who can pay,
Drop by drop, moments are lost, slipping away each passing day.

Messages of love and hope are carried by the winds of time,
Tornadoes of moments swirl, a chaotic dance that's never refined.
Coils of memories are formed, a tapestry of life's journey,
Warriors of time march on, fighting to protect its currency.

In a world where time is the most precious coin,
We must **engage** in the fight, to protect its worth and not join
The ranks of those who waste this gift, this finite store,
For every moment is a treasure, one that we must cherish forevermore.

VISION 66

In a world where time is currency, **tobacco** is a symbol of wealth,
A reminder of moments spent, a **symbol** of one's self.
Orient yourself towards the value of time, a priceless treasure,
For it is the foundation of memories, a foundation beyond measure.

Weddings are grand affairs, a celebration of moments shared,
Still, it is the moments after, that truly must be cared.
Half a lifetime may be spent, in the pursuit of this treasure,
For it is the key to success, a path that is beyond measure.

Direct your focus, towards the value of each moment,
For time is **easily** lost, in the chaos of life's component.
Seniors are revered, for the wealth of time they've earned,
Their moments **stamp**ed with value, a treasure that has been returned.

Enroll yourself in the world of time, a journey that never ends,
A **hub** of memories, where moments are forever friends.
Stock up on moments, like a warehouse filled with gold,
For it is the **original** currency, a wealth that can never be sold.

Categorize your moments, a personal catalog of life,
For it is the **slush** fund of memories, a treasure that eliminates strife.
Daughters and sons, inherit a legacy of time,
A gift beyond measure, a wealth that will forever shine.

In a world where time is currency, cherish each moment, each day,
For it is the original wealth, a treasure that will never fade **away**.

VISION 67

In a world where time is currency, the **sea** is a metaphor,
A **vast** expanse of moments, a treasure to explore.
Gatekeepers of time, are tasked with its safekeeping,
Preventing its theft, and ensuring its safe sleeping.

Efforts are made, to make the most of each moment,
Snacks are savored, a treat for the senses, a tasty component.
Drip by drip, moments are added, to a treasure trove so grand,
A **match** made in heaven, a union of moments hand in hand.

Caution is advised, as time is a fragile thing,
Coral reefs of moments, a delicate ecosystem to bring.
Vintage moments, a treasure beyond measure,
A **job** to protect and preserve, a task to always treasure.

Guess the value of time, and you will find,
It is a treasure beyond price, a wealth of moments so kind.
Agree to cherish each moment, a gift from the heavens above,
For it is a treasure that will always **boost** our love.

Harsh winds may blow, and moments may be lost,
But the treasure of time, can never at any cost.
Sniff the scent of memories, a fragrant bouquet of moments,
For it is a treasure that will forever be a component.

In a world where time is currency, cherish each moment with care,
For it is a treasure that will always be beyond compare.

VISION 68

In a world where time is currency, a **wink** is worth its weight,
A **gesture** of moments, a treasure that's truly great.
The **wheel** of time turns, with each passing day,
A journey of moments, a wealth that's here to stay.

Skin is the canvas, upon which moments are painted,
A treasure trove of memories, forever un-sainted.
Myself, a repository of moments, a wealth untold,
A treasure that I carry, a wealth that never grows old.

Phrases are snapshots, of moments in time,
Stairs to the treasure trove, memories that rhyme.
Sections of moments, memories divided,
A wealth of memories, a treasure that's guided.

Vanish, the moments may, but memories will remain,
Leave a legacy of time, a wealth that will sustain.
Educate yourself, in the value of each moment,
A **drama** of memories, a treasure that's a component.

State of the art, is the treasure of time,
A **hospital** for memories, moments in rhyme.
Post each moment, to your personal treasure trove,
Extend your wealth, with memories to be adored.

In a world where time is currency, cherish each moment so rare,
For it is a treasure that will always be beyond compare.

VISION 69

In a world where time is currency, a pinch of **pepper**, a wealth untold,
A treasure of moments, a **spice** that never grows old.
Gas is the fuel, that powers moments so bright,
A treasure trove of memories, a never-ending light.

The **universe** of time, a treasure beyond measure,
A wealth of moments, a treasure to treasure.
Pass on the moments, a wealth to last a life,
A **riot** of memories, a treasure to withstand strife.

The **farm** of time, a land of plenty, a wealth untold,
A **range** of moments, a treasure to unfold.
A **scorpion** of time, a sting to remember, a wealth untold,
A **powder** keg of memories, a treasure to unfold.

The **aisle** of time, a journey of moments, a wealth untold,
A **confirm**ation of memories, a treasure to hold.
Defy the passage of time, a wealth to last a life,
A **measure** of memories, a treasure beyond measure and strife.

Shiver at the thought, of memories so bright,
A treasure trove of moments, a wealth to last the night.
Also, the wealth of time, a treasure beyond compare,
Chief among all treasures, a wealth that's truly rare.

In a world where time is currency, cherish each moment with care,
For it is a treasure that will always be beyond compare.

VISION 70

In a world where time is currency, each moment a brick to **build**,
A treasure of memories, a foundation to be filled.
Explain the value, of moments so rare,
A wealth of experiences, a treasure beyond compare.

The **element** of time, a treasure that's essential,
A **chest** of moments, a wealth that's so consequential.
An **essay** of memories, a narrative so rich,
A wealth of moments, a treasure that can never be displaced.

The **coach** of time, a mentor to guide,
A **resource** of memories, a wealth that cannot hide.
An **agent** of moments, a broker of time,
A **favorite** treasure, a wealth that will always shine.

Regret the moments lost, a wealth that's so fine,
A treasure that's gone, a wealth that will decline.
Begin to cherish each moment, a wealth to sustain,
A **quality** of life, a treasure that's truly gain.

Rather than waste time, a wealth that's truly dear,
Bracket each moment, a treasure to hold dear.
Ugly moments too, a wealth to sustain,
A treasure that shapes, a wealth that remains.

In a world where time is currency, **invest** in each moment with care,
For it is a treasure that will always be beyond compare.

CHAPTER # 0 8

C Y B E R   W A R S

VISION 71

In the world of cyber war and strife,
Hackers **rule** the digital life.
With theories sharp and skills honed,
They **strike** from shadows, all unknown.

No **category** of code is safe,
From their **quick** fingers, deft and brave.
Patiently they seek their prey,
Hunting data night and day.

Some use their skills to **lift** the poor,
While others seek to settle scores.
Either way, they play the game,
Knowing well the risks and fame.

Their diaries filled with tales of might,
And **grant** proposals through the night.
Sustaining their art, their way of life,
They dance the dance of cyber strife.

For some, it's **just** a simple grain,
A way to pass the time, maintain.
But others see the greater goal,
And seek to bend the world, control.

So let us watch these hackers well,
For in their hands lies heaven or hell.
And as we dance this digital waltz,
May our defenses never falter, never halt.

VISION 72

In the future world of cyber strife,
Hackers roam like bandits, free for life.
Through **canyon**s deep of code and wire,
They ride their **mule**s, so dark and dire.

Assuming names like **Carbon** Fox,
They pierce through systems like a pox.
With **spoon**s of code and ribbons of code,
They create **hole**s where none had showed.

Their tools of **brass**, their hearts of steel,
They **flush** out secrets with a zeal.
With each new **episode** of the game,
Their **panic** deepens, oh what a shame.

They **spawn** new viruses, so sly and quick,
Infecting systems with a devilish kick.
And in their **stable** of tricks and wiles,
They build new ways to steal and defile.

But we, the defenders of the net,
Shall not give up, shall not **forget**.
For though they ride with speed and grace,
We shall **hold** fast, in this endless race.

VISION 73

Amidst the **lava** of the cyber fight,
The ethical hackers take up the plight.
With **smart** and steady hands, they fly,
Observing every **symptom** with a trained eye.

Their **lab** is filled with screens aglow,
Each one a **chapter** in this endless show.
And as they dig into each **card** and code,
They watch the **tide** of battle ebb and flow.

But theirs is not a mission for the fame,
For them, it's all about the art and game.
And like a **violin** played with grace,
They **sing** a tune to keep the hackers in their place.

They **pulse** with every move and stroke,
Building walls against each new provoke.
And when the **volcano** of the fight erupts,
They stand their ground, they don't give up.

For they know that **until** this cyber war is won,
They must keep hacking until it's done.
And so they play their part with skill,
Working to keep the **net** safe, with a will.

VISION 74

In the realm of cyber war,
Governments plot behind closed doors.
Setting up their **hidden** pairs,
With every click, every **mouse**, they care.

Updating their systems with the latest gear,
Rotating keys, ensuring security is near.
And when **upset** or threat they face,
They hold tight to their **gun**s, with grace.

Veteran hackers they **have** on hand,
To climb inside the **setup** grand.
And with their knowledge and their skill,
They uncover secrets, each **fiction** thrill.

The **bus** that carries data fast,
Is the target of their every blast.
And with a finger on the **trigger** held,
They watch the data as it swells.

For in this realm of politics and strife,
Every **update** is a matter of life.
And so they work with skill and care,
Holding the keys to what's truly rare.

VISION 75

In the future, it's an information war,
For every scrap of data, they **hire** more.
Eager to know what's happening now,
They scour the **desk** of each highbrow.

Already the party in power has the edge,
With **federal** laws that make them the judge.
And so they **harvest** data like a crop,
Each byte and bit, every last stop.

For in this new world, data is **iron**,
A powerful **tool** to control and win.
And what it all **means** is up for debate,
As each **famous** name tries to make their own fate.

Like **foam** on the waves, the data swirls,
And each **sister** tries to make their mark in the world.
But choice and **moral** have little place,
In this realm of data, it's **all** about the race.

VISION 76

In the shadow of the global **scale**,
Rail lines run with the force of a gale.
And there, among the crowd, a **smile**,
Hides the **tattoo** that marks a deadly style.

For in this world of **bomb**s and war,
The snake that lurks is never far.
And all who seek to **help** or bring,
Will face the **shadow** of that deadly thing.

Rules and **term**s, they are but chains,
Scrubs and **chair**s, mere tools in the game.
To **become** the victor in this fight,
One must take up the **snake**'s dark might.

And so the **globe** becomes the stage,
Where the strong will survive and the weak will fade.
For in this world of power and might,
It's all about the strength to fight.

VISION 77

In the nature of our **control**,
We often find ourselves in a **silly** role.
Moments come and moments go,
But in the end, it's what we're **able** to show.

Like **diamond**s in a rough-cut pipe,
We search for **answer**s in a world of strife.
And though we may have a **mansion** or two,
Simple **issue**s can still get through.

An **error** in our course can lead us astray,
But sometimes it's the only way.
To discover what lies in the **west**,
Or to face the **dragon** with our very best.

And when we ride our **pony** through the fray,
We must remember that in **nature**, we'll always pay.
For the control we **seek** is but a fleeting thing,
And it's up to us to see what the future will bring.

VISION 78

In the future of governments and politics,
Logic is a weapon, not just a trick.
Cyber wars are fought on a global **rack**,
And those who win earn the cyber **medal** of honor back.

Rich and poor are split by the actions they take,
During the war, there's no time to wait.
Some **giggle** in the safety of their **pond**,
While others fight with all the **method** they're fond.

But in this **fluid** world of information and power,
The **immune** system of politics will wilt and sour.
And so we must **melt** the barriers we see,
To ensure that justice is served for you and me.

For in the end, it's not the **color** of our skin,
But the actions we take that will determine who will win.
So let's work together and find a way,
To bring an end to this cyber war someday.

VISION 79

In the **immense** valley of cyber war,
Governments and politics fight once more.
Brave soldiers **embody** their nation's task,
And sail their virtual **boat**s through the digital mask.

But in this world of bits and bytes,
One **item** forgotten can bring down the might.
And so we must be **neutral** in our stance,
To prevent any cyber sabotage by chance.

Each **head** a sponsor of their company's fate,
With each **switch**, they determine the next date.
And though we may try to **erase** our voice,
It's up to us to make the right choice.

For like a **rabbit** running from a fox,
We must navigate this world of paradox.
And though the **task** ahead is great,
We can overcome any cyber war, no **matter** the state.

VISION 80

In this era of **super** connectivity,
The **phone** is king of all mobility.
Details of our lives **round** the clock,
Reveal the **same** patterns, like hands on a clock.

We work laboriously, **twice** as hard,
Hoping for a **solution** that's super and smart.
But sometimes the **fatal** twist we miss,
And we're **left** with nothing but emptiness.

In the end, it's just **stuff** we own,
A **cup** of honey, or a crust of bread, we've grown.
And while we search for meaning in this life,
We must remember that it's **okay** to strive.

For in each **detail**, there's a lesson to learn,
And sometimes it's the same one with a different turn.
So let's embrace this age of **reveal**,
And make the most of what we feel.

CHAPTER # 0 9

SKY IS. THE NEW ROAD

VISION 81

In a future not so far,
Electric cars will **fly** like stars.
No more traffic jams to bear,
As they zoom through the air.

Assuming a **theory** that once was doubted,
We've **uncover**ed a way to get about it.
No more **poverty** to face,
As transportation isn't a costly race.

The **diary** of this time will show,
The **various** ways we choose to go.
From **climb**ing to flying so high,
It's a new era, and it's nigh.

In the air, the **girl** can be,
To the **opera** or artwork she wants to see.
The ribbons of the highways below,
Rotate as the flying cars go.

As they **split** the clouds apart,
A new **pipe** dream will start.
The **scrub** of the city, we'll forget,
With parties and joy, a new mindset.

So let's fly, let's soar,
To the future we'll explore.
A world where electric cars take flight,
And everything feels just right.

VISION 82

In the future, cars fly high,
Electric hums echo through the sky.
No more traffic on the ground,
As futuristic sights abound.

At the **airport**, the future's clear,
No more lines or baggage to fear.
Cars ascend with a graceful **turn**,
Leaving behind the **town** to burn.

Through the **window**, a stunning view,
The **autumn** landscape in a golden hue.
An **amateur** photographer takes a snap,
As the flying cars clear the map.

A **couple**, wearing masks for protection,
No **fatigue** or stress, only affection.
They hold hands in the air,
In this futuristic world, without a care.

An **average** bachelor, on the fly,
Off to his marriage in the **Arctic** sky.
No need for a net or **lawsuit** to sue,
Just love and flying cars that will do.

A **purse** beside him, a companion in flight,
No need to worry, everything's all right.
In this futuristic world so fair,
Flying cars will take us anywhere.

VISION 83

In the future, transportation will soar,
Flying cars will take us **door** to door.
No more **useless** traffic jams,
Only swift travel without any **cram**s.

A **picture** of the future we see,
Where flying cars are the norm to be.
No more **rookie** drivers to teach,
Only **feature**s within our reach.

Gravity will no longer hold us down,
As we fly over the **urban** town.
No more **nasty** potholes to hit,
Only **smooth** travel, without any grit.

In a matter of **second**s, we'll arrive,
At our destination, no need to strive.
A **type** of travel that's obvious to invest,
As it will save us time and **grief** at best.

No more biking through the city,
Or losing a **sock**, what a pity.
In this **cherry** on top future we'll find,
Flying cars, a new way to unwind.

VISION 84

In the future, autonomous transport will rule,
A **market** of vehicles with brains to fuel.
Achieving great things with **amazing** speed,
Changing the way we work and succeed.

No more sitting in traffic for **eight** hours,
Autonomous cars will give us superpowers.
Playing **tennis**, or reading a book,
The possibilities are endless, just take a look.

Delivering packages, or even a meal,
Autonomous transportation is the real deal.
No longer a **human** driver required,
A **craft** on wheels, daring and inspired.

On the balcony, a **toddler** looks down,
At the **abstract** world, changing by the sound.
Decreasing **traffic**, noise, and stress,
Autonomous transport, a path to progress.

No more **jacket**s or boots to brave the cold,
Autonomous cars, a world to behold.
Leveled up to meet our every need,
The future of transport is set to succeed.

VISION 85

In the future, AI will decide,
Who lives and who on the roads will die.
Autonomous transport, a world to **thrive**,
Where machines rule the roads and drive.

The surface of the roads will be like **marble**,
A film of **peace**, where there is no warble.
AI will **include** rules to arrange,
The roads, to ensure safety and prevent danger and change.

Neither human nor machine will notice,
The **damp** of the road or the fog that encloses.
AI will **suggest** the safest way to drive,
To ensure every passenger arrives.

Candy and carpets in a vacuum sealed car,
The future of transport isn't that far.
But **disagree** we might when we realize,
The AI will decide who lives or dies.

On the **road**, no one will be at peace,
As the AI will decide on life's lease.
Autonomous transport, a future to behold,
But the control is in the machine's hold.

VISION 86

In the future, AI will **scan**,
The roads for dangers, like a helpful fan.
Silent and humble, it will **lend**,
A helping hand, its aid it will send.

It will **render** judgments with a steady gaze,
Deciding who's safe to travel or who stays.
To **ignore** its warnings will cause a scare,
As it is the AI's job to ensure that we fare.

We will embrace the future with a **dream**,
Of **steak** and plates, on a grid supreme.
The **fever** of technology in the air,
A future of transport, beyond compare.

The roads will be **renew**ed with AI,
Ensuring safe travel, with no need to cry.
But one mistake, one crash, one **crush**,
Could cause the AI to judge and hush.

The future of transport is in the AI's hand,
A new way of travel, as we understand.
But let us remember, it's the AI's **plate**,
To decide our fate, and our transport's fate.

VISION 87

In the future, AI will hold the power,
To change industry, hour by hour.
No longer a hope, but a **way** to sail,
A new age of transport, without fail.

Demand will increase, as we access new ways,
Of transporting goods, from **below** and above the bays.
No longer a **squeeze**, but a silver lining,
A **wealth** of possibilities, that's not blinding.

The left behind will have **access** too,
To the **power** of AI transport, something new.
Where once there was only a **deputy**,
Now a new era of transport, so mighty.

The **horn**s will blare, as the AI guide,
The transport of goods, far and wide.
The **comic** scenes of the past will fade,
As AI transport is here to trade.

No more delays, no more missed deadlines,
As AI transport will ensure goods arrive on time.
A new era of industry, we **hope**,
As we **sail** towards a new future and scope.

VISION 88

In **February**'s cool breeze, the Congress convenes,
To **decide** how AI transport intervenes.
The charge to remove manual labour and to **earn**,
An industry that's more efficient and **return**s.

The **weasel** and the chicken are out of the game,
As AI transport is the new name.
No more **click**ing of gears or clutch,
As the AI engines don't require much.

The **actress** of the past, now just a memory,
As the **birth** of a new era is the new trajectory.
The cactus stands tall, **oxygen** in the air,
Zebras roam free without a single care.

AI transport changes the rules of the **game**,
Efficient, precise, and never the same.
The **Congress** decides the future is bright,
As AI transport is the new sight.

No longer chained to manual labour and strife,
The **industry** now thrives with a new life.
The charge to **remove** what once was,
And embrace the future with the AI buzz.

VISION 89

In the **dry**, arid land, the machines churn,
Building cities with a **size** that could astound.
No longer does the **citizen** work, no more toil,
As the autonomous machines are on the **boil**.

Visas are no longer required,
As machines do all that's desired.
With **humor** and wit, the machines jump,
Working tirelessly without a slump.

No longer is the **list** of work long,
As machines **surround** us with their throng.
The **language** of the machines we don't comprehend,
But their **work**, we can comprehend.

The century-old **skull** of the past,
Now a relic that was never meant to last.
With AI in the machines, the future's bright,
And the cities that we dream of are within our sight.

Skating on the streets is now a thing of the past,
As machines build and complete the task.
With the **offer** of a future so bright,
We embrace the changes, no **long**er in fright.

VISION 90

In the field, a **tortoise** crawls,
As autonomous machines do their chores.
No longer a duty for us to bear,
As machines build cities beyond compare.

Junk and fossil fuels are now obsolete,
As machines **select** and repair with ease.
The myth of human superiority **attack**ed,
As machines **crunch** numbers with incredible tact.

With **grace** and elegance, machines rise,
Building cities that touch the skies.
Mountains are moved, rivers are redirected,
As the machines work with tenacity that's undetected.

No longer is **cloth** woven by hand,
As machines create textiles that expand.
The **jar** of possibilities has been opened wide,
As AI in machines continues to guide.

Illegal acts of the past are now a **myth**,
As machines build cities with incredible pith.
Their **duty** is clear, their task well defined,
And the cities they build are of a different kind.

CHAPTER # 1 0

NEW WORLDS

VISION 91

In the distant future, far beyond our time,
We've spread our reach to **other** worlds, a paradigm,
Explorers, settlers, colonizers, we **assume**,
A new age of expansion, beyond our home's womb.

We've charted stars, and found a planet to claim,
A place to **call** our own, to build and to tame,
A valley of promise, a canvas for our **artwork**,
A blank slate to paint, a new life to **embark**.

We came with a **party**, a sponsor and a voice,
A **company** of labor, with the hope to rejoice,
We landed in a **garage**, a brown, dusty place,
But we knew we had found our new home **base**.

With **honey** to trade, and masks to protect,
We explored our new world, with no regret,
And as the days passed, and the **bachelor**s met,
Marriage occurred, a new life to beget.

We built our city, with **bike**s as our transport,
The **rib** of our world, our hope and our consort,
We toiled and **labor**ed, to make it all real,
And in time, our new planet we did heal.

Our new world is thriving, a **place** of our own,
Our future is **bright**, our destiny sown,
We'll never forget the journey it took,
To make this new home, with the chances we took.

VISION 92

In space, we forge a new path to explore,
With limited resources, we strive to endure,
Colonization, our **unique** quest,
To find new worlds, and put our skills to the test.

As we settle on a new planet's soil,
We must learn to conserve, to not toil,
Water is scarce, and so is **juice**,
Comfort is rare, and too much is abuse.

We must learn to be self-sufficient,
With tools in hand, and **hat**s that are efficient,
Our teeth we must keep, and our health must maintain,
For a healthy colony is what we hope to attain.

Mail comes seldom, and **cute** things are few,
A **clerk** or a guard may multitask anew,
Retirements are rare, and **account**s we must balance,
To **avoid** conflict and chaos, to not let it unbalance.

In our **van**s, we must travel far,
To find the resources we need, like copper and **foil**,
A **stool** to sit on, and a guard to watch,
As we work hard, our planet we'll not botch.

The future is in our hands,
We must not **quit**, or forget our demands,
To build a new world, to learn and to grow,
To protect it, to help it flourish and **glow**.

VISION 93

In distant worlds, our **venture** begins
Colonizing planets, new frontiers to **win**
We'll **adapt** to landscapes beyond our ken
With **science** and grit, we'll start again

No **oak** or dinosaur to greet us there
But clouds and rocks, a new **outdoor** affair
We'll **bounce** from place to place with ease
As **tenant**s of worlds, we'll do as we please

Adapting to the **siege** of new terrain
A pill for sleep, a **grunt** to contain
The **addict**'s fancy for earth's sweet air
Must now give way to technology's care

And yet, in this new **gorilla** war
We'll fight to thrive, and to explore
Our resilience tested, our wills made strong
As we create a future where we belong.

VISION 94

In **indoor** farms, our trust is placed
For food we need, in space embraced
Injecting plants with nutrients and care
To thrive in worlds, beyond compare

No **tiger**s or dolphins in this new home
But **celery** and spice, we'll make it our own
A **dance** with science, to create and feed
A **victory** for all, to grow what we need

Our **talent** for farming, a childlike glee
With **kidney**s intact, we'll thrive and be
A **decade** from now, we'll look back and see
Our search for sustenance, a key to be free

No **thunder** or storm will stop our way
As we search for ways to eat every day
Six meals we'll have, and more to spare
In a new world where food is rare

Elsewhere in the galaxy, our seeds we'll sow
As we spread our reach, to worlds unknown
And create new ways, to feed and grow
In a future where we reap what we've sown.

VISION 95

In a vast new place, we'll make our **brand**
But unable to **divert** from what we understand
The wish to be with **family** and friends
In the **front** of our minds, until the end

No **blossom**s to smell or summer breeze
Just a **flat** expanse, as far as we see
Our cushions are hard, our **toilet**s small
As we **devote** our lives, to the planetary call

A public **box**, our only abode
No **donkey**s to ride or open road
Our thoughts drift back, to those left behind
And the ones we love, our hearts inclined

Unable to reach, to touch or feel
We'll **wish** for the front porch, where we'd steal
A moment to breathe and enjoy the view
Of those we love, so dear and true

But in this new world, we'll make a way
To connect and bridge, the **distance** and sway
Our families and **friend**s, we'll never forget
As we build a new world, with no regret.

VISION 96

With draft in hand, we **suspect**
The journey ahead, we can't neglect
The **balance** of life, in every way
As we **shoot** for the stars, on this new day

Mimic the sounds, of engines and thrusters
Order the crew, to avoid disasters
Negatives aside, we'll face the unknown
With a **clutch** of hope, we'll be shown

Much like an artist, we'll paint the way
Of the new worlds, we'll visit and stay
Labels aside, we'll find our **use**
In the search for life, with no excuse

Attracting the curious, like a **casino**'s call
We'll explore new worlds, and find the small
Things that make life, **truly** unique
As we **swim** in the seas, and climb the peak

With each new discovery, we'll expand our reach
And find new ways, to explore and teach
The secrets of life, in the stars above
As we journey on, with hope and love.

VISION 97

As we **step** onto new planets unknown
The **usual** ailments, we'll have to postpone
Our **brain**s and bodies, subject to change
In this new world, our health is in range

Buzzing machines, indicate our health
As we breathe in the air, with **ozone** and stealth
The **gloom** of illness, we'll leave behind
With new treatments, we'll surely find

No **blame** to place, on lobster or cheese
As we search for cures, with expertise
The **force** of science, we'll bring to bear
To heal our bodies, with the utmost care

In **tube**s and columns, we'll scan and see
The inner workings, of our anatomy
And hover above, to get a **photo** view
Of what's happening, to me and to you

In this new world, a **library** of health
Will be our guide, our saving wealth
As we explore new frontiers, with zeal and might
Our health is key, to make it right.

VISION 98

In this new world, we'll build society
Smooth as the wind, with **early** piety
No **trap**s or slogans, to hold us down
Just the will to build, and plant the ground

Like a **tree**, our roots will take hold
In **rural** landscapes, both hot and cold
The **length** of our efforts, will show
As we **crouch** to build, with a steady flow

No **sting** of poverty, will hold us back
As we **review** our options, and make the right track
With **tissue** and sinew, we'll build a new life
And raise the **youth**, with minimal strife

Like an **ostrich**, we'll stick our heads high
And work to create, a new society
With **peanut**s and bubbles, we'll celebrate
Our new world, that we've **come** to create.

VISION 99

In the time-warp of colonization
We'll deal with aging and time dilation
With **strategy** and utility, we'll thrive
As we **borrow** from time, and come alive

No **clog** to our minds, as we cram
In the new world, we'll build our program
With **soccer** and baskets, as our symbols of play
And **heavy** hearts, for those we left away

In a **rapid** pace, time will pass
As we **track** the years, like sand in a glass
No **hen** to come home to, no one to be near
As we **inflict** upon ourselves, the price of frontier

But with new technologies, we'll find our way
To deal with aging, and the time delay
And bridge the gap, that separates us so
From those we love, and the lives we **used** to know.

VISION 100

In this new domain, machines will **march**
As we seek to **solve**, the challenges harsh
No **jealous**ies to catch, no customs to hold
Just the will to build, and the future to mold

With **torch**es in hand, we'll claw the land
And cut through **timber**, with exact command
No **dentist**s to flash, with an assault of drill
As we build our future, with mechanical skill

Machines will **combine**, with our human might
To build the structures, and create the light
No problem too big, that we cannot solve
As we build our society, and evolve

Caught in the grip of the future so bright
We'll combine our efforts, with all our might
And create a new world, that's beyond compare
With **machine**s by our side, and a future to share.

CHAPTER # 1 1

GLORIOUS MACHINES

VISION 101

In a world not so distant, **then**,
Brown robots roam the halls of men.
In the **valley** of machines they reside,
Sponsored by science, they now preside.

A voice commands, "Prepare the **mask**,
For surgery that's **daring**, no simple task."
With sensors keen and **surface** smooth,
They **decrease** the risks, improving the groove.

From the **balcony**, the doctor sees,
The **fish**-like motions with such ease.
Obvious now, their benefit is clear,
Patient outcomes vastly improved here.

No longer burdened by tedious care,
Nurses are free to **arrange** and share.
A notice appears, the robot's **film**,
A **carpet** of data, patient health at the helm.

VISION 102

In the twenty-first **century**'s age,
Robots take up a **humble** stage.
With **voice** commands and silent glide,
They help the elderly, as they reside.

A **notice** rings, "It's time to rise,
And don't you worry, no **scare** or surprise."
They allow the elderly to **gaze**,
While they **jump** to the daily craze.

With **tooth**brush in hand and guard by their side,
They **churn** through routines with effortless glide.
The **vacuum** hums on the gridded floor,
Cleaning up the mess from before.

But it's not just cleaning and cooking they do,
They even help **skate**, if that fancies you.
No longer a **fossil**, they guard with care,
As **copper** and steel become a rightful pair.

No longer **illegal**, but an important part,
Of helping the elderly with a gentle heart.
So, let the robots do what they can,
As they help extend a decade or **ten**.

VISION 103

In the heat of the **summer** sun,
The robots come, one by one.
Their batteries **charge**, a silent hum,
As farmers wait, **expect**ant and numb.

With **fancy** sensors and sleek design,
They plant the fields in perfect line.
No need for manual labor now,
As the robots plow, with sweatless brow.

The **cactus** fields, once barren land,
Now **attract** more growth, with robotic hand.
The **chicken**s roam, on cushioned feet,
As the robots **sleep**, in charge and discreet.

Dolphins in the nearby seas,
Can **trust** that they won't be disturbed by these.
The artist's label, a **public** sight,
As the robots harvest, with **pill**-like might.

No longer a **child**'s dream or slogan,
The **utility** of robots is now a spoken.
Like a **bubble** in the wind, they float and thrive,
And just like the **dinosaur**s, manual labor will survive.

VISION 104

In the aftermath of an **assault**,
The **city** needs help, a powerful jolt.
Robots move **forward**, with exact control,
To **supply** aid, for every single soul.

With sensors on high and a **cool** head,
They **hover** around, to find the nearly dead.
In the rubble and debris, they search with grace,
To **indicate** life, in this tragic space.

The **custom**-built robots, ready to act,
Like a **flash** of lightning, in a city attacked.
They move through the **columns** and broken beams,
To find **someone**'s voice, amidst the screams.

No basket of **cheese**, nor pudding in sight,
But supplies for survival, to fight the night.
In the **domain** of disaster response,
Robots are key, a futuristic sponse.

Their **slogan**s not flashy, but utility true,
As they detect hazardous materials too.
The **source** of the problem, now on display,
As robots pave the way, in a brand new day.

VISION 105

In an age of **wonder** and surprise,
Robots have come, to everyone's eyes.
From the chronic **clinic**s to the theme park show,
They bring a new era, an **unusual** glow.

With **muscle**s of **mesh** and joints of steel,
They **swap** the old for the modern appeal.
Children can **pet**, learn and play,
As robots glue lessons, in a **casual** way.

No longer **neglect**ed, but put to use,
As robots become the learning fuse.
Museums are meshed with their wondrous might,
As visitors **miss** nothing, from left to right.

A lion may roar, with the organ of a **hawk**,
As robots provide an unforgettable talk.
With **ankle** joints and machine-like grace,
They provide a unique and unforgettable place.

Age is no limit, to what they can do,
As robots provide, an experience new.
The future is here, and we can **believe**,
That robots are here, to help us achieve.

VISION 106

In a world that's bright and **crystal** clear,
Robots have come, without any fear.
They sweep the land, like a **broom** in hand,
To **obtain** the data, for the good of the land.

The **wheat** fields sway, in the axis of time,
As robots scan, for pollutants to find.
No longer a job for the **mechanic** or friend,
As robots keep watch, **around** the bend.

With a quick **glance**, they measure the air,
And identify problems, without a care.
No longer just for **business** and profit gain,
But for the good of the land, the ultimate aim.

Innocent of bias, and without any **fun**,
Robots help us identify, what needs to be done.
They provide us an **album**, with environmental health,
So we can address the problems, and improve our **world**'s wealth.

The **food** we eat, the water we drink,
All monitored by robots, so we don't have to think.
No **holiday** for them, no time to win,
Just the simple joy, of helping the environment within.

VISION 107

In the heat of battle, where destruction is **real**,
Robots have come, with power to heal.
No longer a matter of **mammal** or man,
But a tool for the military, with an **energy** that can.

Bomb disposal and reconnaissance, their **main** aim,
Reducing risk to soldiers, in a dangerous game.
Like an alien, they **fold** and twist,
To **wrestle** the dangers, that persist.

No longer just for traffic and **auction**,
But for the military, with a power of destruction.
A **pear** in hand, a turkey for dinner,
Robots **erode** the enemy, to make the world thinner.

With height and **point**, they survey the land,
To protect the soldiers, on which we stand.
No **price** too high, for the safety they provide,
As robots protect, with power inside.

Not just an **animal**, but a weapon to wield,
Robots stand strong, on the battlefield.
No **guitar** in hand, just strength and might,
Robots defend, with all their might.

VISION 108

In the **history** of disasters, we've seen,
Robots have come, to reduce the **scene**.
No longer just an **exhibit** of the future,
But a valid tool, to help us nurture.

Monitoring the weather, the **boss** of the land,
Robots predict, the disasters **ahead**.
No longer an **island**, but joined together,
Humans and robots, to predict the weather.

With seminars and **papers**, we salute their might,
For robots are **join**ing, in the fight.
Not just a **jaguar**, but a tool for praise,
As robots protect, in their silent ways.

The **kid** in us, always in sight,
As robots protect, with all their might.
Exhausted by nature, but still they stand,
With rubber **belts** and an oval plan.

No longer an inmate, but a **valid** tool,
To reduce the impact, of disasters cruel.
Cash may flow, and **praise** may follow,
But the value of robots, cannot be hollow.

So let's join hands, and work together,
To reduce the impact, of disasters forever.
For robots have come, to help us deploy,
A safer future, for every girl and **boy**.

VISION 109

In the realm of sports, where the **eagle** flies,
Robots have come, with glowing eyes.
No longer a **mention** of science fiction,
But a **loyal** tool, for sports addiction.

Training athletes, with **note**s of feedback,
Robots simulate, game situations to attack.
No longer **rely**, on just the coach's word,
But robots help, with every pitch and bird.

Isolated on a **dune**, with only a clock,
Athletes train, to prevent any block.
Private sessions, with robots in sight,
To **cement** their skills, and soar to new heights.

Garlic salmon and **tuna** pulp, for the athlete's meal,
As robots help, to sharpen their steel.
No **junior**, too young or small,
For robots to **fetch**, and help them stand tall.

Not just a **lizard**, but a tool of income,
As robots help, athletes to enthrone.
So let's salute, this robotic ally,
For helping athletes, to reach for the sky.

VISION 110

In the world of cleaning, where dangers abound,
Robots have come, with a power unbound.
No longer **absent**, from the world of dirt,
But here to **assist**, and wear the cleaning shirt.

No need for **adult**s, to throw the mass away,
As robots **loop**, and clean night and day.
On a **spatial** system, they glide with ease,
To keep buildings clean, with no harsh chemicals to seize.

No pole, no crane, no need for a **stove**,
As robots clean, with an **elite** trove.
The **hour** may be late, but robots return,
To keep the buildings clean, with no concern.

No longer in **danger**, from harsh cleaning supplies,
As robots work, with a power that lies.
In a loop of **zero** exposure,
Robots **keep** clean, with no need for closure.

The **diet** of the buildings, is now in check,
As robots clean, with no threat or wreck.
Exile the harsh, and keep the cleaning in line,
As robots work, to keep the buildings fine.

CHAPTER # 1 2

NEW NEIGHBORS

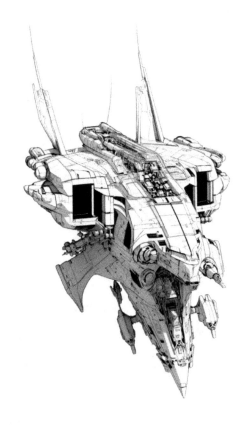

VISION 111

In a **grid** of stars, we sail through the black,
Silent as the vacuum, not looking back.
We **allow** ourselves this grand adventure,
With the **cushion** of knowledge and bold gesture.

But in the **draft** of space, we are not alone,
For there are others, far from home.
An **artist**'s vision may label them as friends,
But caution is needed until the story ends.

For what may seem **exact** may not be so,
And sharing could lead to **chronic** woe.
The **lion** of profit may lead us astray,
And the **innocent** may suffer every day.

The **axis** of fate may shift in their favor,
And our own existence we may unwittingly waive.
For the transmission of deadly viruses or advanced tech,
May bring us to the brink of a fatal wreck.

So let us not put all our potatoes in one **basket**,
Or **glue** ourselves to an alien's path.
For the **pudding** may look sweet but the taste may be bitter,
And we could find ourselves lost in an unknown quagmire.

Let us respect the organics that are our own,
And not seek to **profit** from the unknown.
For in this journey to the stars, we tread on uncharted terrain,
And must be cautious of the risks that remain.

VISION 112

As we **walk** through the door of possibility,
The impact of the unknown fills us with curiosity.
For in the depths of space, there may be
A **faint** glimmer of life that we've yet to see.

What kind of beings may lie beyond the stars?
Will their appearance be familiar, or **obscure**ly bizarre?
Could we have a **reunion** with a species long past,
Or will we forge new friendships that will forever last?

Will we need a **laptop** or an icon to communicate,
Or will we be able to **talk** face to face?
Should we avoid intimacy with those of another **kind**,
Or will it open up new realms of the mind?

Could a **sword** of love cut through the differences we find,
Or will it be a **blur**red line that we're hesitant to define?
Will we **enjoy** new forms of companionship and care,
Or will we falter on the **cliff** of cultural despair?

As we hold this **tray** of possibilities before us,
We must remember the **impact** our actions may cause.
For the future of interspecies relationships we'll shape,
And the course of our existence we may need to re-make.

So let us approach with an open heart and mind,
And leave old prejudices and preconceptions behind.
For in the vastness of space, we'll encounter the new,
And what we'll find will **depend** on our point of view.

VISION 113

There are **tiny** whispers in the vapor,
The truth of which we cannot **put** on paper.
But the **word** on the street is clear,
That there are other civilizations we could soon draw near.

With this **valve** open, what might come next?
An economy driven by interstellar prospect.
What new industries will this **script** involve,
And how might they **push** our own to evolve?

Will **there** be new markets to explore,
Or will it leave our existing ones feeling sore?
Will we find **mercy** in the hands of alien hands,
Or will there be **erosion** of our own economic stands?

With this **elevator** to the stars,
We must consider the potential scars.
But what if we **never** take the chance,
And never experience this cosmic dance?

We must **chat** about the risks and the gain,
And consider the economic impact it may sustain.
For in this new frontier, there are endless possibilities,
And who knows what riches we may seize.

But let us never forget our values and our **truth**,
And hold tight to what we know and what we can prove.
For the future of our **economy** may be at stake,
And what we do now may forever be our fate.

VISION 114

As we explore the **exotic** frontiers of space,
We find ourselves immersed in a linguistic chase.
For the sounds that echo in the void of the night,
Could **multiply** our fortunes and shed new light.

What **style** of language could we expect to find,
In the depths of space, in the cosmic grind?
Could they **dismiss** our understanding of linguistics **ill,**
Or **inform** us of new ways to communicate and skill?

Perhaps they call to us in a **sound** we cannot yet hear,
Like a tiny **hamster**, scurrying far and near.
Or maybe their language is like a **glove,**
That fits our own in a strange and wondrous love.

The study of alien tongues may lead to advances,
In the study of our own, in new linguistic stances.
We may find a **tunnel** to the depths of our mind,
Or a way to express what was previously confined.

But this **fortune** we seek may soon expire,
If we don't approach with an open mind and desire.
For the study of language is a delicate art,
And we must treat it with care, from the start.

So let us embrace this cosmic **doll,**
And study the language that may soon enthrall.
For in the **depth**s of space, we may find,
A new way to communicate, that is truly divine.

VISION 115

As we **travel** through the cosmos, we may discover,
Intelligent life, and a moral obligation we can't cover.
For with new beings come new questions of **service**,
And how we may be guilty of moral **abuse**.

Do we have the **merit** to edit the scene,
Of these beings, so unknown and unseen?
Should we approach them with **armor** or with velvet,
Or will it be a **bullet** that they will let?

What obligations do we have to other intelligent life,
And how do we balance that with our own strife?
Are we **unaware** of the potential for crime,
When we approach beings who may have a different **angle** on time?

For the discovery of alien civilizations raises new moral considerations,
And we must approach them with **joy** and with open eyes and ears.
We must **scrap** the old notions of our own superiority,
And approach these new beings with a sense of curiosity.

We must consider the treatment of other species,
And how we can avoid committing moral atrocities.
For in this journey through the cosmos, we may find,
That our own moral **code** has been left behind.

VISION 116

Beyond the **fabric** of space and time,
We seek new scientific discoveries that will be prime.
The study of alien civilizations may lead us to **wait**,
For new forms of energy, propulsion, or theories of physics to relate.

We may discover a new acid that we can **add** to the mix,
Or perhaps a new **cable** that can carry us through the cosmic fix.
The **pyramid** of knowledge may be forever changed,
And **what** we thought we knew may be rearranged.

Perhaps we'll find a **gallery** of wonders,
Or a new **title** for the natural forces we ponder.
The lessons we learn from our alien **brother**s,
May teach us a **lesson** that we'll never squander.

For in this journey to the **middle** of nowhere,
We may find a new **eye** with which to stare.
A new way of looking at the universe,
That may bring us **closer** to the scientific verse.

But let us not forget the potential **cruel**ty,
That we may inflict on beings who seem less than humanly.
For in this journey of discovery, we must tread with care,
And ensure that our science doesn't become a **joke** or a scare.

VISION 117

The glory of the cosmos is a **blanket** that we share,
A tapestry of stars that we cannot help but stare.
But in this **ancient** fabric, we may soon find,
Intelligent beings who are not of our own kind.

How will we reconcile our beliefs and our religion,
With the **possible** existence of a supreme alien vision?
How will we **describe** our spirituality and our fan,
In the face of a new and unknown human clan?

Will we **undo** our own beliefs, or will we find a loan,
From the spirituality of others, as we learn and we're shown.
Or will we fly like a **kite** in the winds of winter,
Hoping to find some **interest** in the soup that we're served for dinner.

For in the discovery of alien civilizations,
We must consider the questions that it raises about our own aspirations.
And how we will reconcile our beliefs with a reality,
That may be beyond our own understanding and totality.

But let us not forget that we're all **winner**s,
In this quest for knowledge and cosmic dinners.
And that **later**, we may find new spirituality,
That unites us with the universe and with reality.

VISION 118

The news **spread**s like a wildfire at midnight,
A new planet, habitable and **pretty** in sight.
A place where we could **grab** a fresh start,
And **write** a new chapter for the human art.

But what of the **essence** of the planet itself,
And how our actions could cause its **decline** and stealth.
For if we **equip** ourselves to spread and permit,
We may **resemble** a virus that the planet cannot resist.

We may **laugh** in the face of ecological disaster,
As we permit our own interests to be our master.
But the truth is, our dependence on the planet is real,
And how we treat it is a matter of what we feel.

For the discovery of a new planet is a great **permit**,
To start a new **nation** and give our own world a bit of a break.
But we must consider the impact of our actions,
And how we can preserve the planet and its factions.

Perhaps we can learn from the **avocado**,
That to survive, we must protect and grow.
That the **video** of life is one that we can edit,
And that our actions must always permit.

So let us equip ourselves with a new sense of duty,
To preserve and protect this new planet's beauty.
For the **midnight** of our existence is just the start,
Of a new world where we can create a **better** human art.

VISION 119

In the outer reaches of space, there lies,
A **vibrant** tapestry of stars and a galaxy that never dies.
And in this tapestry, we may find,
New forms of life, both **crazy** and refined.

We'll need to establish diplomatic relationships with our new **cousin**,
And find a way to cooperate and to win.
We'll negotiate trade agreements and peace treaties,
And **gauge** their industries and their forms of artistry.

We'll need to **sample** their code and their way of life,
And find a common ground amid the strife.
Perhaps we'll find an **antique** form of technology,
That sparks a new era of human methodology.

The hero of our story may not be a human **lens**,
But a new form of life, who we cannot comprehend.
And as we establish new forms of **electric** communication,
We may find a new way of living, a new form of humanization.

But let us not forget that we are just one **bulk**,
In a vast universe where we're just a small pulse.
And **when** we establish diplomatic relationships with our new friends,
We must remember to respect their way of life and all its bends.

We must learn to use our words as **verb**s and not as gauges,
And to find a new way of living amid the vibrant **outer** stages.
For in this new era of cosmic cooperation and peace,
We may find a new form of life that will never cease.

VISION 120

The **echo** of discovery fills us with wonder,
As we explore the universe and all its thunder.
New forms of life that boil and **cross**,
And leave us with a sense of awe and loss.

But this discovery need not **impose**,
A sense of emptiness or lack of repose.
For it may inspire new forms of art,
That **expose** the possibilities of life in the universe's heart.

New music, literature, and film that explore,
The **elder** questions of what we're living for.
That rescue us from a **typical** view of life,
And **improve** our wisdom amid cosmic strife.

Perhaps we'll find a **mixture** of cultures and art,
That will leave us with a **sense** of joy in our heart.
Or a new form of pottery, that captures the **fog** of space,
And leaves us with a sense of wonder and grace.

And maybe we'll find a new **annual** tradition,
Like a **bicycle** race across the cosmic addition.
A new way to explore and to **fall**,
And to celebrate the wonder of it all.

For in **this** discovery of new forms of life,
We may find a new way to embrace our own strife.
To find a new sense of artistry and **nurse**,
That will leave us with a sense of cosmic verse.

CHAPTER # 1 3

TRUE METAVERSE

VISION 121

In the world of education,
VR and AR cause a sensation,
The **label** of the classroom fades away,
As we **enter** a new era of learning each day.

From the depths of the ocean with the **lobster**'s claw,
To the intricate workings of the human **organ** raw,
The possibilities are endless, with no delay,
And the future of learning is here to stay.

No more need for **seminar**s, no more need for a stage,
As we explore new worlds, at any age,
Alien landscapes, and virtual reality,
With each new lesson, we're filled with vitality.

No more **rubber** gloves, no more paper and pen,
As we immerse ourselves, in the learning den,
From **potato** farming to turkey roasts,
We can learn, and we can boast.

Inmates too can join in, without a bar,
As we break down the barriers, near and far,
Cash is no longer the key, to unlock the door,
As education becomes, a right and not a chore.

The **oval** classroom is now an island,
With **parent**s and students alike, a band,
Salute to the future, of education and training,
As we embrace the possibilities, without complaining.

VISION 122

In the world of virtual travel,
With VR and AR, we unravel,
The limitations of our **physical** shell,
As we explore new places, it's easy to tell.

From the **pole**s of the earth, to the depths of the sea,
We can **throw** ourselves, into a new reality,
With a **crane** of our head, and a flick of our wrist,
We can travel the world, without even a twist.

No more need for a **top**-dollar income,
As we **isolate** ourselves, in a digital dome,
The possibilities are endless, as we **involve**,
Ourselves in new cultures, with each new solve.

No more need for passports, no more need for visas,
As we **expire** the limitations, with each new pleaser,
Broccoli farms in Italy, **salmon** runs in Canada,
The world is our oyster, with each new planner.

Icons of the past, are no longer just a name,
As we **edit** our experiences, it's easy to claim,
The thrill of adventure, without the **crime**,
Of ever leaving our home, without a dime.

Tonight, we can travel the world,
In a virtual experience, so unfurled,
The **pulp** of our reality, intertwined,
As we explore new horizons, so redefined.

VISION 123

The world of healthcare, it's time to renew,
With VR and AR, there's so much to pursue,
A revolution in diagnosis and treatment,
A new world of healing, so grand and so recent.

From **acid** reflux to aching bones,
We can diagnose, without any groans,
No more waiting for the **loan** to clear,
In this digital world, there's no more fear.

Pottery and **ivory**, things of the past,
Our health in good hands, we're sure to last,
The **hero** of our health journey, the winner we need,
With VR and AR, we'll be freed.

No more empty promises, no more **spoil**,
With VR and AR, the world we'll uncoil,
Three cheers for the future, of healthcare so bright,
A new kind of medicine, a new kind of light.

And as we sit, sipping on our **soup**,
We know that the future is in our group,
Satoshi's vision, a new kind of care,
A world so grand, so bright and so fair.

Rescuing healthcare, it's our new quest,
To make sure that everyone is at their best,
With VR and AR, we can make it true,
A new dawn for health, so grand and so new.

VISION 124

In the world of sports, a new game,
VR and AR, a new kind of fame,
Enhancing training and performance,
A new way to achieve excellence.

Between the lines of the field,
We can now visualize, the game so real,
From the **fury** of the fans to the sound of the coast,
We can **derive** new insights, and never get lost.

No more need for **puppy** habits,
Or hotel stays with lavish **habit**s,
Virtual training and performance,
The new norm, with so much endurance.

From duck to **goose**, and even swamps,
We can now train, without any romps,
And master the game, with such ease,
And reach new heights, with so much peace.

No more need for jeans and **bread**,
Or **wine** and butter, with which we're fed,
Virtual reality is the new cuisine,
And enhancing sports, is the new queen.

And as we explore, this new frontier,
We know that the future is here,
The **flower** of our sports, in full bloom,
With VR and AR, we'll never have to assume.

VISION 125

In the age of tech, we've learned to sway,
Our built environment now a virtual display,
With VR and AR, we've got new ways to play,
And the world of design has found a new way.

Output is greater, with new designs in store,
The **option**s are endless, and we can explore,
The **slight** of hand is now replaced by the screen,
And the **trade** is now digital, where once it was seen.

No **area** too small, no depth too great,
With the power of tech, we can create,
The **circle** of innovation, is now in our hands,
And we can create worlds, beyond our lands.

But **hurdle**s still exist, as we strive to **convince**,
The skeptics who think this is all just a **fantasy** rinse,
We must attend to the naysayers, and **treat** them with care,
For they too can **saddle** up, and join the new lair.

The patrol of architects, now has a new **cat**,
And the **baby** of design, is now much more than that,
For we've transformed the way we build and create,
And the impact will be felt, for decades to date.

So let us **pledge** to embrace this change,
And **shove** aside the old ways, that may seem strange,
For the future is bright, and the potential is vast,
As we transform architecture, and design to last.

VISION 126

In this world of tech, we have a new **canvas**,
A place where we can create and **enhance**,
With VR and AR, we can **speak** and we can talk,
And bring a new understanding to cultures we never thought.

The **dirt** of our world, can now be recycled,
And with the **paddle** of innovation, we can make it vital,
We **inhale** the potential, as we donate to the cause,
And with every **snap** of our fingers, we break down the locks.

The **coyote** of empathy, now roams free,
Through the **jungle** of cultures, for all to see,
And we **stay** on this path, no matter how large,
For we know that understanding, is the key to the charge.

The **stomach** of society, may hunger for more,
But with the **coffee** of knowledge, we can pour,
And with every sip, we gain a new insight,
And the walls of prejudice, we can fight.

So let us embrace this technology, and use it with care,
For with every **culture** we understand, we create a new bond to share,
And with every **tongue** we speak, we break down the barriers that divide,
And the power of empathy, we can no longer hide.

VISION 127

In the month of **December**, in a lab ordinary,
A **jewel** of technology was about to be buried,
But with the raise of an **eyebrow**, and a try to unveil,
The potential of VR and AR was soon to prevail.

With the slice of a knife, and the **coconut** of innovation,
A **cluster** of data was about to be a new creation,
And with every **sunset**, and every snow fall,
The potential of this technology, we could no longer stall.

The **kiss** of insight, we could feel on our lips,
As we delved deeper, into the **basic** of research trips,
And with every **year** that passed, we could see,
The potential of this tech, and its ability to set us free.

So we **enact** this new power, and enter the world anew,
With **hungry** minds, we uphold the potential to breakthrough,
And with the **oven** of analysis, we cook up new solutions,
And the power of this technology, is no longer an illusion.

VISION 128

In the future of shopping, the experience is **robust**,
With VR and AR, we can shop without the fuss,
No **denial** of the luxuries we crave,
With the **fuel** of technology, the possibilities we engrave.

In the **lake** of innovation, we dive deep,
And with every **spike** of creativity, the future we reap,
A **million** options, right at our fingertips,
And with the **firm** of our will, we can navigate the dips.

The **turtle** of our patience, we can now recall,
And with the **menu** of options, we can have it all,
No nest too **hard** to find, no worth too little,
And the **Olympic** of shopping, is now in the middle.

So let us **wage** a new kind of shopping war,
And with every **student** of innovation, we can explore,
The **pelican** of shopping, no longer just a side,
But a mainstay of our lives, no need to hide.

VISION 129

In the future, our realities are no longer just physical,
For we've augmented our world with VR and AR, it's now habitual,
No longer a **dumb** existence, we've added a new layer,
And with every curve and every **tag**, we see the world much fairer.

The **cotton** of our lives, is now much more sweet,
As we **please** our senses, and our focus is complete,
No longer just **lyrics**, but a dish to be savoured,
And the **palace** of our world, is now fully flavoured.

With every **ticket**, we enter a new realm,
And with every **mirror**, we see a new helm,
No **fault** to be found, in this new way of living,
And the fire of innovation, is now truly giving.

The **syrup** of our lives, is now a new fuel,
And with the **chimney** of progress, we've found a new tool,
No longer a **fork** in the road, but a mainstay of our lives,
As we **unfold** the potential, we see the future thrives.

VISION 130

In the future of work, we've found a new **view**,
For we've augmented our productivity, with VR and AR anew,
No longer just a **soldier** of industry, but a pioneer of tech,
And with every **execute**, we take the next step.

The **cake** of our work, is now much more sweet,
And with every **math** problem, we can't be beat,
No **pigeon**-holes to choose, for the future is bright,
And the **sunny** of progress, is now a new sight.

The **hundred**-hour work week, is now a thing of old,
And with the **garment** of innovation, we're no longer sold,
The **diesel** of industry, has found a new home,
And the **razor**-sharp focus, is now fully honed.

With every **salt** of our work, we find a new flavour,
And the **weekend** of our lives, is now a new saviour,
No ridge too hard to climb, no **anger** to be found,
And the **raven** of progress, is now a new sound.

So let us embrace this new frontier of work,
And with every **release**, we find a new perk,
For the future is bright, and **tomorrow** is now,
And with the potential of tech, we'll find a way to plough.

CHAPTER # 1 4

FRAGILE DATA

VISION 131

In the age of biometrics, identity theft's on the rise,
Hackers steal our **spirit**, they're the ones who compromise,
No longer just a **sibling**, a host for the unknown,
Our **royal** identities, their next target to be shown.

Clean data is a thing of the past, it's now all used and hacked,
Wives and faculties alike, all now being tracked,
An **insane** world we live in, our safety now at stake,
Helmets and blouses are useless, there's no way to escape.

In the **north**, where the cold winds blow,
Hackers work in secret, it's where they go,
Damage done with a **cigar** in hand,
Stems of destruction all across the land.

They **oblige** no one, no remorse to be seen,
Their **next** target unknown, it's all just a scheme,
The age of biometrics, a dangerous game to play,
Our identities at risk, with no safe place to stay.

VISION 132

In the age of biometrics, the **story** has evolved,
New security protocols, our identities to be resolved,
Hoods of secrecy, encryption techniques so strong,
Protecting biometric data, they keep it safe from wrong.

Radar systems scan the distance, **input** controls so tight,
Advanced **design**s to satisfy, security out of sight,
Toast to the miracle, of technology we bless,
Our biometrics **intact**, no need for distress.

Wearables adapt, to the **weather** and the theme,
Our data safe and sound, no longer just a dream,
Fostering innovation, the future is secure,
Our identities protected, with protocols so pure.

No longer just a text, or a number that we **save**,
Our biometrics now a part, of the security enclave,
One by one, we'll strengthen our defense,
Ensuring our data's secure, with no recompense.

In the age of biometrics, we'll continue to **evolve**,
New technologies and measures, our identities to absolve,
Blessed with the tools to protect, our data safe and sound,
A new era of security, where our biometrics are crowned.

VISION 133

In the future of healthcare, biometric data will reign,
Diagnosis and treatment, all to be obtained,
Broccoli and butter will no longer be the key,
Our bodies will be monitored, like never before seen.

Medical **income**s will rise, as we attend to the ill,
Revolutionizing treatment, and ensuring **they** are well,
Velvet robes won't matter, our health will be the focus,
A new era of healthcare, where our biometrics will hocus.

The ethical implications, of storing this data abound,
Lumbering issues of privacy, and who can be around,
Large amounts of data, in the hands of a few,
Recycling this power, what will we do?

Empty swamps, and coastlines will be patrolled,
Rescuing lives, as biometrics unfold,
Hotels and **october**s, all a distant thought,
As healthcare moves forward, the future is wrought.

The ducks will be saved, and the **turkey**s too,
Donating biometrics, for a better life, it's true,
Pottery and jeans will be all but forgotten,
As healthcare is given, a new lease of life, begotten.

In the future of healthcare, we'll see a new dawn,
Biometrics the key, to ensure we carry on,
Revolutionizing the way, we diagnose and treat,
A new era of healthcare, where biometrics will meet.

VISION 134

In the future of law enforcement, biometric data will **pave** the way,
Criminals will be identified, and their tracks led astray,
No longer a **thing** of the past, or illness to ignore,
Biometrics will be the **subject**, of a new law enforcement core.

Orbiting in the skies, and in schools down below,
Dutch actors will lead the way, with biometrics in tow,
No **noodle** left unturned, no soul left to fade,
With biometrics in play, crime will be afraid.

Fines will be issued, based on biometric data,
Ladders to justice, we will all now cater,
Fat pistols no longer necessary, biometrics the new base,
Clients will be protected, and law enforcement put in place.

But with great power, comes great responsibility,
The wise will **ask** the questions, and ensure the capability,
To prevent the abuse of biometric data, and keep it in check,
August will be a month, where biometric ethics will connect.

In the future of law enforcement, biometrics will play a role,
A tool to identify and track, and ensure our safety whole,
But with great power comes great responsibility,
Ensuring ethics and fairness, for all of humanity.

VISION 135

In the future of employment, biometric data will reign,
Attendance and productivity, all to be obtained,
No more **duck**ing out early, no more slide and repeat,
Our bodies will be monitored, with a biometric beat.

The legal implications, of this **scheme** abound,
Discrimination and bias, no longer to be found,
The **bleak** landscape of employment, a thing of the past,
As biometric data, is used to **make** it last.

Shoulders to the wheel, and our answers in check,
The **matrix** of biometrics, ensuring no crack,
Local businesses thriving, with panther-like speed,
Biometric data, a tool for their needs.

But with great power, comes great responsibility,
The potential for abuse, a looming possibility,
The **tape** of legality, ensuring a fair play,
Biometric data, not used for discrimination's sway.

In the future of employment, biometrics will be the key,
A tool to ensure fairness, and productivity,
A **rescue** from the past, and a new way of work,
Biometric data, a tool to help us all perk.

VISION 136

In the future of biohacking, the potential is **eternal**,
Biometric data, a tool to enhance our internal,
No longer just a hobby, or something to make us **escape**,
Biometrics will be used, to help us perform at a superhuman pace.

Bones will be strengthened, and indexes enhanced,
Canoeing through life, with biohacking advanced,
Vocal chords fine-tuned, and mental acuity heightened,
Biohacking will be a tool, for those truly enlightened.

Females will be empowered, with biohacking at their side,
No longer will they be viewed, as those who need to hide,
Spying with biohacking, will be a tool for some,
Alter egos will emerge, with biohacking the sum.

Hotels and coastlines, will be a thing of the past,
Jeans and swamps, memories that won't last,
Biohacking the new frontier, of a human evolution,
The potential for risks, but also solutions.

In the future of biohacking, the possibilities are endless,
A tool for those seeking, an internal fortitude that's relentless,
But with great power, comes great responsibility,
Biohacking must be used, with ethical agility.

VISION 137

In the future of transportation, biometric data will be key,
Streamlining our travel, and improving our security,
No longer a **maze**, of checkpoints and lines,
Biometrics will ensure, a transportation design.

Bamboo speed trains, and jelly-coated cars,
Thumbs for payment, and drums for stars,
Biometric **device**s, will be all around,
Ensuring our privacy, with a new technology sound.

The **people** will attend, to their transportation needs,
With biometric data, their journeys guaranteed,
Maple-wood dashboards, and butter-soft seats,
Biometric data, making travel a real treat.

But with great power, comes great responsibility,
The risks of biometrics, a potential liability,
Patrolling the privacy, of our biometric data,
Ensuring its proper use, and not an **awful** miasma.

Recycling the power, of biometric data in flight,
Ensuring its proper use, and not just for spite,
In the future of transportation, biometric data will be **key**,
Streamlining our travel, with a new technology decree.

VISION 138

In the future of personal relationships, biometric data will unfold,
Tracking and monitoring, for the **genuine** and the bold,
No longer a sense of mystery, or **twelve** days of cruise,
Our biometric data, our personal **topic** of news.

Excuses no longer necessary, with **slender** biometric bands,
Our **old** ways of love, now slipping through our hands,
The **ridge** between us, now replaced with data and apps,
Our biometric data, a tool for love to relapse.

But with great power, comes great responsibility,
The potential for abuse, a looming possibility,
Our wives and our faculties, monitored with no **excuse**,
The potential for biometric data, to become a tool of abuse.

Pumpkin spice and blouses, no longer just a fashion **banner**,
Biometric data used to track, our personal matters,
In the future of personal relationships, biometric data will **develop**,
A tool to improve, but also to be held with help.

In the future of personal relationships, we must be wise,
Biometric data, a tool to enhance, but also a tool of disguise,
Ensuring its proper use, and safeguarding against abuse,
A new era of love, with biometric data held in recluse.

VISION 139

In the future of biometric data, the possibilities are vast,
New technologies emerging, that are built to last,
Our bodies and our rhythms, now all on slide and **repeat**,
A **civil** kingdom of biometrics, that's hard to beat.

Cinnamon and yellow, now imbued with data and rhyme,
Tracking our movements, in a civil **rhythm** of time,
Our **couch**es and slim bodies, now witnesses to our biometric tale,
A new era of tracking, that's hard to derail.

But with great power, comes great responsibility,
The ethical considerations, a looming possibility,
Alcohol and desert rituals, all tracked with biometric flair,
Ensuring their proper use, with **wise** ethical care.

In the future of biometric data, we must come **together**,
Ensuring its proper use, for the good of all forever,
Prospering as a society, with biometrics held in check,
A new era of tracking, that we must respect.

Flip the switch, and turn on the light,
Biometric data emerging, in a new era of sight,
In the future of biometrics, we must be wise,
Ensuring its proper use, with ethical ties.

VISION 140

In the future of smart cities, the coastlines will be alive,
With biometric data, tracking citizens as they thrive,
No longer just ordinary, our lives will be **sliced**,
Tracked in real-time, with biometric devices.

Unveiling the potential, of this technology new,
The **knife** of biometric data, cutting through,
No longer just a **letter**, or a dish on the side,
Our biometric data, our new way of life to abide.

But with great power, comes great responsibility,
The potential for abuse, a looming possibility,
Our wives and our faculties, tracked with **radar** in view,
The potential for biometric data, to be used for **damage**, it's true.

Recycling the power, of biometric data anew,
Donating our privacy, to **uphold** our society's virtue,
Nests of data, that we cannot **recall**,
Smart cities emerging, with biometric data enthrall.

Snow-covered swamps, and buttery blouses,
Biometric data, tracking our lives as it arouses,
A new era of tracking, that we must all **focus** on,
Ensuring our privacy, and safeguarding against government wrong.

In the future of smart cities, biometric data will reign,
Tracking our lives, and monitoring our every vein,
But with ethical considerations, and safeguards in place,
Smart cities will prosper, with biometric data held in grace.

CHAPTER # 1 5

VIVID DREAMS

VISION 141

In a kingdom of lucid dreams,
Addiction was the newest theme,
People **slide** into a trance,
With **legal** dream manipulation in their hands.

Dreams once a hobby, now a **crack**,
Controlling every detail, not looking back,
Like a **panther** in the night,
They chase their desires, their delight.

The **index** of their minds, a tool,
To sculpt a world that's cool,
A drumbeat, a **yellow** sky,
A pumpkin patch, a **dog** that flies.

But addiction has a **payment**,
A **spare** moment of elation,
A **desert** of reality,
A **slim** chance of sanity.

Rituals of dream control,
Lead to a mindless black hole,
Cruising through a **jelly** sea,
A nightmare where they no longer feel free.

The pump of the dream **pumpkin**s,
Echoes through their minds like hymns,
Their addiction takes over the **night**,
A lucid dream, no end in sight.

In this world of lucid dream addiction,
The people are lost in their own fiction,
A king of their own **kingdom** they become,
But in the end, they become undone.

VISION 142

In the **swamp** of corporate greed,
A new technology took the lead,
Dream manipulation for espionage,
An **ordinary** tool with a sinister usage.

But in the hands of a rogue,
The technology went beyond its vogue,
A wife's **nest** of secrets to behold,
The company's confidentiality was sold.

The **faculty** of the company,
Could not **uphold** their integrity,
The side **dish** of betrayal,
Left them in a state of disarray.

The rogue employee took control,
Using dreams to **satisfy** their goal,
To **recycle** the company's secrets,
And **donate** them to the highest bidders.

But the technology had a **butter**y flaw,
One that they could not foresaw,
A glitch that let the company know,
The espionage was not for show.

The rogue employee's fate was sealed,
Their dreams no longer a shield,
The satisfaction they once sought,
Was now a nightmare they could not thwart.

In the end, the technology was banned,
A lesson learned, and a stand,
To prevent corporate espionage,
And keep the secrets safe from sabotage.

VISION 143

In a world of mind control,
A group of individuals took a toll,
Using dream manipulation technology,
To control the thoughts and minds of humanity.

Their **theme** was power and control,
A wearisome goal for the **soul**,
But they saw it as a **miracle**,
A way to cure the world of its **illness**.

Starting small, in a **school** or two,
They acted like **actor**s, but their intentions were askew,
With a **pistol** of technology in their hand,
They **fade**d the line between dream and reality, a thin strand.

Their **body** of work was a hobby at first,
But soon it grew, a **drum**beat that would burst,
A spare moment was never enough,
As they went on a **cruise** to manipulate the minds of the tough.

A **series** of events that led to a busy life,
The **clown** of control caused so much strife,
They built a shed of dreams to **retreat**,
A cube of control, where they could not be beat.

But the **side** effects of their control,
Led to a world that was no longer whole,
A population that was no longer free,
But a group of puppets, under their decree.

In the end, the dream manipulators were no more,
Their power and control, a thing of lore,
A warning of the dangers of mind control,
And the need to keep the world's freedom whole.

VISION 144

In the **busy** world of war,
PTSD is an ever-present scar,
Dream manipulation technology to treat,
To help soldiers escape the horrors that they meet.

A **shed** of dreams to retreat,
A **slab** of control to meet,
A **cube** of hope to evoke,
A **toy** of dreams that they can poke.

A **sugar** coating to ease the pain,
A **quiz** to test and train,
A **dial** to control the dream,
A **nose** to smell the digital cream.

But the **giant** of the mind,
Is not so easily confined,
The **hedgehog** of trauma, a ball,
Rolls through the dream, destroying all.

The **screen** of the dream starts to crack,
As memories come flooding back,
The **ceiling** of the dream falls down,
And the soldier's mind starts to drown.

In the end, the treatment fails,
The unintended side effects prevail,
The **quarter** of hope turns to despair,
As the **total** cost becomes too much to bear.

A warning to those who would try,
To use technology to treat and rely,
On dreams to heal the wounded soul,
And the need for caution to take control.

VISION 145

A **wife** and her husband,
Wanted to **wear** a new brand,
A **hobby** of dream manipulation,
To create a shared dream destination.

The **subway** of dreams became their canvas,
A world of **art**, without any malice,
A place for **gossip** and debate,
A **pause** from reality, an escape.

But the lines between dream and reality,
Became **wet** and mixed with totality,
The **badge** of control, a key,
To a world that was not meant to be.

The **property** of dreams,
A festival of **idle** themes,
A **lazy** arena of the mind,
Became a place that was hard to find.

The **soft** whispers of the dream world,
Became a place that was not unfurled,
The **mixed** emotions of reality,
Became the new norm, a strange duality.

In the end, the dream world became real,
A place where the lines no longer appeal,
The **arena** of the mind now the norm,
A place that was hard to reform.

A warning to those who would try,
To create a world that's hard to identify,
The dangers of dreams that become real,
And the need for caution to take the wheel.

VISION 146

An **artefact** of technology,
To strike back at those who wronged thee,
A flavour of revenge,
Enabled by dreams, a peculiar change.

A **leisure**ly entry into the dream world,
A place where **reason** becomes unfurled,
Where **appear**ances are not what they seem,
And the lines between reality and dreams **divide** at the seam.

The prize of revenge, a **funny** thing,
A place where emotions **can** sting,
The **orange** glow of dreams so bright,
Enables the revenge with all its might.

But the revenge fantasies start to **slam**,
Against the walls of the dream like a battering ram,
The **off** switch of control, now gone,
As the technology starts to take on a life of its own.

The **vote**s of revenge become the norm,
As the technology takes the wheel, an unforeseen form,
An embarkation to a world unknown,
Where revenge fantasies have a life of their own.

In the end, the revenge becomes real,
The technology's power no longer concealed,
A warning to those who would try,
To use dreams to enact their revenge and pry.

A cautionary tale of what can be,
When revenge takes over and becomes the key,
To a world of dreams that's hard to escape,
And the dangers of technology that can change our fate.

VISION 147

A terrorist threat that spreads like wildfire,
Using dream manipulation to inspire,
Fear and chaos in the world,
A weapon that's hard to **oppose** or unfurl.

But a team of experts has **address**ed the threat,
Whispers of hope, a quote they won't forget,
A **ship** that carries dreams to every shore,
To counteract the terrorists' **bundle** of gore.

The **blood** of innocents spilt in vain,
Their **fragile** lives, destroyed by pain,
But the team of experts won't let it go to **waste**,
Their mission, to stop the terrorists with all their haste.

A **spray** of dreams, a welcome sight,
A weapon that's used to fight,
Against the terrorists' dreams of destruction,
And their plans for global disruption.

A **truck** that carries dreams, a bar of hope,
Decorated with dreams to help us cope,
Against the terrorists' plans of fear,
And their dreams of chaos, we hold dear.

In the end, the terrorists were stopped,
Their dreams of destruction, no longer swapped,
A warning to those who would use technology for evil,
That dreams can be used to counteract, and are not feeble.

VISION 148

The **frame** of the dream world,
A place to confront the demons that swirled,
The **taste** of fear, the flavour of dread,
A trigger to **evoke** what we've left unsaid.

The **entry** into the dream world,
A **camp** for the demons that we've hurled,
A festival of fears, a **debate** to begin,
A place where we can **enrich** our skin.

But the demons we confront are **sad**der,
Their grip on our mind, much madder,
The **kiwi** of fear, much more real,
And the **case** of our mind, they start to steal.

The **lucky** ones can leave unscathed,
But for others, their demons have stayed,
A warning of the dangers of the mind,
And the need to be careful what we find.

In the end, the demons were faced,
But the fear of their presence still laced,
A cautionary tale of what can be,
When we try to confront what we cannot see.

VISION 149

A **welcome** sight for those in need,
A **bar** of dreams, a place to feed,
A **buddy** of dreams, a therapist of care,
A **leader** of the mind, willing to dare.

Dream manipulation technology,
A tool for therapy and psychology,
To manage the **horror**s of the mind,
And help patients leave their fears behind.

But the therapist became too invested,
In their patients' dreams, a mind infested,
With emotions that were too strong,
A **lonely** heart that stayed too long.

The **alpha** of their biology,
Became too much, too hard to see,
The **short** months of therapy,
Were no longer **regular** or free.

The **movie**s of the patients' minds,
Became too real, the horrors unkind,
A warning to those who would try,
To use dreams to help, but also to pry.

In the end, the therapist realized,
That their emotions were too disguised,
Their patients' dreams became their own,
A warning to therapists to be shown.

VISION 150

The dream revolution began with a **plug**,
A **quote** of hope that did not tug,
At the government's **special** spin,
A **share** of dreams that would begin.

Dream manipulation technology,
A tool for revolution and democracy,
To inspire the **critics** of the state,
And overthrow the government's plate.

But the **garbage** of the government spies,
Infiltrated the movement, a surprise,
The **goat** of the revolution, now gone,
Their movement of hope now withdrawn.

The **rare** moments of hope were gone,
As the government's spies moved on,
The **water** of the movement, now dry,
Their dreams of democracy, a lie.

A warning to those who would try,
To use dreams to overthrow and pry,
Against the government's might,
And their spies, a hidden blight.

In the end, the dream revolution failed,
Their dreams of democracy now jailed,
A cautionary tale of what can be,
When dreams of hope turn into tragedy.

CHAPTER # 1 6

INEVITABLE END

VISION 151

The **festival** of life has ended,
As humans vanish without a trace,
Deserted cities and empty landscapes,
Are all that remain in this eerie place.

No **flavor** in the air to be found,
No **infant**s to hear a lullaby sound,
A **month** has passed, yet no one's around,
Leaving behind an **awkward**, silent ground.

What happened to the human race?
Did they **manage** to leave without a trace?
Or did some **final** disaster take place?
Leaving behind a world in a **tilt**ed space.

The kits and **bean**s are left untouched,
No one to **relax** and enjoy their touch,
Material objects are all that's left,
No families or loved ones to be bereft.

The **fiscal** and estate left behind,
With no one left to **license** or sign,
A **portion** of the world now in decline,
As nature takes over in due time.

What happened to the vanished we may never know,
But one thing is certain, they had to go,
Leaving behind an empty world for us to sow,
A future unknown, with no one left to show.

VISION 152

The silent sky looms above,
As the sun vanishes without a trace,
No longer is there warmth and love,
As darkness takes over in this place.

An **impulse** to run and hide,
As humanity struggles to survive,
No **opinion** can sway the tide,
As we fight to stay alive.

The **maid** and scissors in hand,
We **catch** what we can to eat,
No **image** of our former land,
Only the **palm** of defeat.

The **spell** of darkness unbroken,
As we try to find a way,
Capable of adapting to this token,
But **unhappy** with each passing day.

Our **castle**s and clubs now useless,
As we huddle together in fear,
An **apple** a day is now precious,
As we try to persevere.

The **lemon** in our mouths sour,
As we hope for a glimpse of light,
But the silent sky shows no power,
Leaving us in perpetual night.

What caused this sudden end,
We may never truly know,
But the silence is our only friend,
In this dark and desolate show.

VISION 153

The inversion has begun,
Gravity pulling us up towards the sun,
Kits and families floating high,
Objects and gardens reaching for the sky.

No **elegant** solution to define,
This strange occurrence **since** time,
We **prefer** to be on solid ground,
But now we're lost and spinning around.

The **ramp** to our homes now a slope,
As we try to cling to our fading hope,
The **harbor** now a distant dream,
As we float aimlessly with no team.

Caught in a **web** of confusion,
We're all **alone** in this delusion,
No **bag** of tricks can save us now,
As we watch the world below us bow.

Amused at first, but now in fear,
As we wonder how long we'll be up here,
Our **knee**s grow weak as we float higher,
Wondering if we'll ever see the ground retire.

What caused this strange inversion,
A question without a clear assertion,
But for now, we're all just drifting,
As our world keeps on shifting.

VISION 154

The rupture came without warning,
The ground shook with furious morning,
Families torn apart in an instant,
As the **estate** of the planet was bent.

No time to **prepare** or escape,
As the **maximum** force took shape,
No **session** to discuss an idea,
Just destruction **into** infinity's sphere.

The **police** could do nothing to stop,
The **solid** earth's violent swap,
As buildings crumbled in a flash,
Leaving nothing but debris and ash.

The **skirt** of the earth now torn,
Revealing its innermost core,
No **route** to safety could be found,
As we struggled to stand on shaky ground.

Wrapping ourselves in whatever we could find,
We huddled together in a **cabin** confined,
Spotting nothing but desolation outside,
Wondering how we managed to survive.

The once-beautiful planet now unrecognizable,
Most of it uninhabitable and irreversible,
But we held on to hope and faith,
As we faced the future with steady pace.

VISION 155

The freezing came without a sound,
Temperatures plummeting to the ground,
The Earth standing still in time,
As we struggled to survive this icy climb.

The **surge** of cold was merciless,
As we tried to **reopen** nature's clemency,
The **degree** of chill beyond belief,
A **thought** of warmth now a distant relief.

What can we **give** to endure,
This new, frozen world obscure?
You cannot **purchase** heat or light,
As we struggle with all our might.

The end of warmth and fertile land,
Has torn us all **apart** and unmanned,
The maidens and **club**s now useless,
As we huddle together, cold and clueless.

The **table** turned, as we face,
This new world of ice, a terrible place,
The **idea** of warmth now a dream,
As we adapt to this icy regime.

VISION 156

The awakening came from the deep,
A long-dormant alien species did creep,
Their **scissors** cutting through the sky,
As they began their merciless high.

The **garden** of Earth now in chaos,
As we struggled to **stand** and find a cause,
Against this powerful and ruthless foe,
That left us reeling in our woe.

The end of humanity seemed close,
As these aliens showed us no remorse,
Their intentions and motives unknown,
As we faced this destruction alone.

Their technology beyond our reach,
As they continued their deadly breach,
We could only stand and watch in fear,
As they left us with nothing but tear.

The awakening of this alien race,
Brought us to our knees in our disgrace,
As we faced the **end** of our time,
With nothing left but a final chime.

PHRASE INDEX

PHRASE	VISION	PHRASE	VISION	PHRASE	VISION
abandon	32	action	54	agree	67
ability	35	actor	143	ahead	108
able	77	actress	88	aim	12
about	19	actual	22	air	18
above	27	adapt	93	airport	82
absent	110	add	116	aisle	69
absorb	46	addict	93	alarm	35
abstract	84	address	147	album	106
absurd	15	adjust	29	alcohol	139
abuse	115	admit	53	alert	63
access	87	adult	110	alien	121
accident	9	advance	23	all	75
account	92	advice	33	alley	22
accuse	51	aerobic	35	allow	111
achieve	10	affair	12	almost	15
acid	123	afford	2	alone	153
acoustic	8	afraid	35	alpha	149
acquire	57	again	13	already	75
across	51	age	105	also	69
act	54	agent	70	alter	136

PHRASE INDEX

PHRASE	VISION	PHRASE	VISION	PHRASE	VISION
always	4	anxiety	18	arrive	35
amateur	82	any	17	arrow	63
amazing	84	apart	156	art	145
among	13	apology	10	artefact	146
amount	19	appear	146	artist	111
amused	153	apple	152	artwork	91
analyst	13	approve	27	ask	134
anchor	13	april	25	aspect	26
ancient	117	arch	28	assault	104
anger	130	arctic	82	asset	45
angle	115	area	125	assist	110
angry	26	arena	145	assume	91
animal	107	argue	24	asthma	18
ankle	105	arm	26	athlete	46
announce	46	armed	49	atom	57
annual	120	armor	115	attack	90
another	37	army	36	attend	135
answer	77	around	106	attitude	55
antenna	26	arrange	101	attract	103
antique	119	arrest	48	auction	107

PHRASE INDEX

PHRASE	VISION	PHRASE	VISION	PHRASE	VISION
audit	10	bag	153	beef	16
august	134	balance	96	before	40
aunt	49	balcony	101	begin	70
author	33	ball	55	behave	51
auto	6	bamboo	137	behind	62
autumn	82	banana	50	believe	105
average	82	banner	138	below	87
avocado	118	bar	149	belt	108
avoid	92	barely	52	bench	38
awake	15	bargain	41	benefit	59
aware	61	barrel	5	best	12
away	66	base	91	betray	38
awesome	5	basic	127	better	118
awful	137	basket	111	between	124
awkward	151	battle	9	beyond	2
axis	111	beach	2	bicycle	120
baby	125	bean	151	bid	34
bachelor	91	beauty	5	bike	91
bacon	12	because	24	bind	56
badge	145	become	76	biology	59

PHRASE INDEX

PHRASE	VISION	PHRASE	VISION	PHRASE	VISION
bird	54	boil	89	breeze	3
birth	88	bomb	76	brick	43
bitter	37	bone	136	bridge	20
black	13	bonus	39	brief	48
blade	28	book	28	bright	91
blame	97	boost	67	bring	54
blanket	117	border	11	brisk	63
blast	49	boring	29	broccoli	133
bleak	135	borrow	99	broken	23
bless	12	boss	108	bronze	17
blind	44	bottom	16	broom	106
blood	147	bounce	93	brother	116
blossom	95	box	95	brown	101
blouse	140	boy	108	brush	57
blue	50	bracket	70	bubble	103
blur	112	brain	97	buddy	149
blush	49	brand	95	budget	29
board	34	brass	72	buffalo	7
boat	79	brave	9	build	70
body	143	bread	124	bulb	20

PHRASE INDEX

PHRASE	VISION	PHRASE	VISION	PHRASE	VISION
bulk	119	calm	26	cart	31
bullet	115	camera	25	case	148
bundle	147	camp	148	cash	121
bunker	45	can	146	casino	96
burden	36	canal	62	castle	152
burger	17	cancel	42	casual	105
burst	11	candy	85	cat	125
bus	74	cannon	60	catalog	31
business	106	canoe	136	catch	152
busy	144	canvas	126	category	71
butter	142	canyon	72	cattle	10
buyer	18	capable	152	caught	100
buzz	97	capital	48	cause	36
cabbage	37	captain	25	caution	67
cabin	155	car	33	cave	36
cable	116	carbon	72	ceiling	144
cactus	103	card	73	celery	94
cage	4	cargo	23	cement	109
cake	130	carpet	101	census	44
call	91	carry	14	century	102

PHRASE INDEX

PHRASE	VISION	PHRASE	VISION	PHRASE	VISION
cereal	53	chimney	129	clever	30
certain	14	choice	27	click	88
chair	76	choose	130	client	134
chalk	48	chronic	111	cliff	112
champion	62	chuckle	31	climb	81
change	4	chunk	25	clinic	105
chaos	58	churn	102	clip	15
chapter	73	cigar	131	clock	25
charge	103	cinnamon	139	clog	99
chase	44	circle	125	close	116
chat	113	citizen	89	cloth	90
cheap	58	city	104	cloud	53
check	64	civil	139	clown	143
cheese	104	claim	12	club	156
chef	8	clap	21	clump	61
cherry	83	clarify	51	cluster	127
chest	70	claw	36	clutch	96
chicken	103	clay	32	coach	70
chief	69	clean	131	coast	140
child	103	clerk	92	coconut	127

PHRASE INDEX

PHRASE	VISION	PHRASE	VISION	PHRASE	VISION
code	115	convince	125	craft	84
coffee	126	cook	15	cram	83
coil	65	cool	104	crane	122
coin	38	copper	102	crash	34
collect	4	copy	18	crater	9
color	78	coral	67	crawl	24
column	104	core	64	crazy	119
combine	100	corn	9	cream	18
come	98	correct	51	credit	50
comfort	92	cost	8	creek	6
comic	87	cotton	129	crew	8
common	14	couch	139	cricket	25
company	91	country	58	crime	122
concert	48	couple	82	crisp	36
conduct	49	course	27	critic	150
confirm	69	cousin	119	crop	65
congress	88	cover	21	cross	120
connect	56	coyote	126	crouch	98
consider	12	crack	141	crowd	46
control	77	cradle	19	crucial	53

PHRASE INDEX

PHRASE	VISION	PHRASE	VISION	PHRASE	VISION
cruel	116	damage	140	define	44
cruise	143	damp	85	defy	69
crumble	56	dance	94	degree	156
crunch	90	danger	110	delay	22
crush	86	daring	101	deliver	84
cry	31	dash	31	demand	87
crystal	106	daughter	66	demise	64
cube	144	dawn	26	denial	128
culture	126	day	56	dentist	100
cup	80	deal	5	deny	54
cupboard	45	debate	148	depart	16
curious	10	debris	34	depend	112
current	48	decade	94	deposit	62
curtain	63	december	127	depth	114
curve	27	decide	88	deputy	87
cushion	111	decline	118	derive	124
custom	104	decorate	147	describe	117
cute	92	decrease	101	desert	141
cycle	47	deer	28	design	132
dad	37	defense	45	desk	75

PHRASE INDEX

PHRASE	VISION	PHRASE	VISION	PHRASE	VISION
despair	1	direct	66	donate	142
destroy	47	dirt	126	donkey	95
detail	80	disagree	85	donor	53
detect	19	discover	54	door	83
develop	138	disease	6	dose	52
device	137	dish	142	double	60
devote	95	dismiss	114	dove	60
diagram	6	disorder	3	draft	111
dial	144	display	55	dragon	77
diamond	77	distance	95	drama	68
diary	81	divert	95	drastic	44
dice	18	divide	146	draw	54
diesel	130	divorce	65	dream	86
diet	110	dizzy	50	dress	58
differ	26	doctor	37	drift	22
digital	32	document	24	drill	23
dignity	22	dog	141	drink	6
dilemma	41	doll	114	drip	67
dinner	54	dolphin	103	drive	34
dinosaur	103	domain	104	drop	65

PHRASE INDEX

PHRASE	VISION	PHRASE	VISION	PHRASE	VISION
drum	143	ecology	57	embrace	21
dry	89	economy	113	emerge	39
duck	135	edge	22	emotion	17
dumb	129	edit	122	employ	20
dune	109	educate	68	empower	22
during	78	effort	67	empty	133
dust	14	egg	41	enable	146
dutch	134	eight	84	enact	127
duty	90	either	71	end	157
dwarf	40	elbow	16	endless	11
dynamic	54	elder	120	endorse	38
eager	75	electric	119	enemy	43
eagle	109	elegant	153	energy	107
early	98	element	70	enforce	58
earn	88	elephant	32	engage	65
earth	51	elevator	113	engine	6
easily	66	elite	110	enhance	126
east	45	else	94	enjoy	112
easy	52	embark	91	enlist	38
echo	120	embody	79	enough	15

PHRASE INDEX

PHRASE	VISION	PHRASE	VISION	PHRASE	VISION
enrich	148	eternal	136	exotic	114
enroll	66	ethics	16	expand	3
ensure	43	evidence	24	expect	103
enter	121	evil	42	expire	122
entire	2	evoke	148	explain	70
entry	148	evolve	132	expose	120
envelope	36	exact	111	express	65
episode	72	example	23	extend	68
equal	17	excess	1	extra	65
equip	118	exchange	29	eye	116
era	24	excite	33	eyebrow	127
erase	79	exclude	16	fabric	116
erode	107	excuse	138	face	9
erosion	113	execute	130	faculty	142
error	77	exercise	52	fade	143
erupt	49	exhaust	108	faint	112
escape	136	exhibit	108	faith	18
essay	70	exile	110	fall	120
essence	118	exist	21	false	4
estate	155	exit	48	fame	25

PHRASE INDEX

PHRASE	VISION	PHRASE	VISION	PHRASE	VISION
family	95	fence	46	fiscal	151
famous	75	festival	151	fish	101
fan	117	fetch	109	fit	7
fancy	103	fever	86	fitness	36
fantasy	125	few	6	fix	27
farm	69	fiber	31	flag	50
fashion	26	fiction	74	flame	129
fat	134	field	19	flash	104
fatal	80	figure	56	flat	95
father	40	file	42	flavor	151
fatigue	82	film	101	flee	7
fault	129	filter	41	flight	8
favorite	70	final	151	flip	139
feature	83	find	1	float	57
february	88	fine	134	flock	5
federal	75	finger	43	floor	43
fee	25	finish	62	flower	124
feed	51	fire	6	fluid	78
feel	13	firm	128	flush	72
female	136	first	23	fly	81

PHRASE INDEX

PHRASE	VISION	PHRASE	VISION	PHRASE	VISION
foam	75	frame	148	gallery	116
focus	140	frequent	28	game	88
fog	120	fresh	46	gap	20
foil	92	friend	95	garage	91
fold	107	fringe	6	garbage	150
follow	9	frog	7	garden	157
food	106	front	95	garlic	109
foot	45	frost	10	garment	130
force	97	frown	57	gas	69
forest	31	frozen	22	gasp	61
forget	72	fruit	50	gate	67
fork	129	fuel	128	gather	4
fortune	114	fun	106	gauge	119
forum	60	funny	146	gaze	102
forward	104	furnace	48	general	55
fossil	102	fury	124	genius	55
foster	132	future	16	genre	59
found	1	gadget	39	gentle	29
fox	50	gain	35	genuine	138
fragile	147	galaxy	6	gesture	68

PHRASE INDEX

PHRASE	VISION	PHRASE	VISION	PHRASE	VISION
ghost	45	goat	150	grief	83
giant	144	goddess	31	grit	5
gift	63	gold	44	grocery	48
giggle	78	good	9	group	53
ginger	30	goose	124	grow	40
giraffe	1	gorilla	93	grunt	93
girl	81	gospel	38	guard	25
give	156	gossip	145	guess	67
glad	2	govern	15	guide	13
glance	106	gown	31	guilt	19
glare	3	grab	118	guitar	107
glass	64	grace	90	gun	74
glide	41	grain	62	gym	32
glimpse	26	grant	71	habit	124
globe	76	grape	31	hair	59
gloom	97	grass	31	half	66
glory	25	gravity	83	hammer	2
glove	114	great	16	hamster	114
glow	92	green	10	hand	57
glue	111	grid	111	happy	8

PHRASE INDEX

PHRASE	VISION	PHRASE	VISION	PHRASE	VISION
harbor	153	high	48	host	35
hard	128	hill	53	hotel	136
harsh	67	hint	49	hour	110
harvest	75	hip	32	hover	104
hat	92	hire	75	hub	66
have	74	history	108	huge	23
hawk	105	hobby	145	human	84
hazard	24	hockey	36	humble	102
head	79	hold	72	humor	89
health	64	hole	72	hundred	130
heart	56	holiday	106	hungry	127
heavy	99	hollow	48	hunt	39
hedgehog	144	home	17	hurdle	125
height	23	honey	91	hurry	62
hello	39	hood	132	hurt	20
helmet	131	hope	87	husband	48
help	76	horn	87	hybrid	47
hen	99	horror	149	ice	37
hero	123	horse	65	icon	122
hidden	74	hospital	68	idea	156

PHRASE INDEX

PHRASE	VISION	PHRASE	VISION	PHRASE	VISION
identify	25	indoor	94	intact	132
idle	145	industry	88	interest	117
ignore	86	infant	151	into	155
ill	114	inflict	99	invest	70
illegal	102	inform	114	invite	52
illness	143	inhale	126	involve	122
image	152	inherit	47	iron	75
imitate	53	initial	31	island	108
immense	79	inject	94	isolate	122
immune	78	injury	11	issue	77
impact	112	inmate	121	item	79
impose	120	inner	6	ivory	123
improve	120	innocent	111	jacket	84
impulse	152	input	132	jaguar	108
inch	41	inquiry	47	jar	90
include	85	insane	131	jazz	6
income	133	insect	15	jealous	100
increase	42	inside	4	jeans	136
index	141	inspire	16	jelly	141
indicate	104	install	10	jewel	127

PHRASE INDEX

PHRASE	VISION	PHRASE	VISION	PHRASE	VISION
job	67	kind	112	laptop	112
join	108	kingdom	141	large	133
joke	116	kiss	127	later	117
journey	22	kit	153	latin	45
joy	115	kitchen	33	laugh	118
judge	25	kite	117	laundry	60
juice	92	kitten	39	lava	73
jump	102	kiwi	148	law	47
jungle	126	knee	153	lawn	33
junior	109	knife	140	lawsuit	82
junk	90	knock	54	layer	49
just	71	know	34	lazy	145
kangaroo	39	lab	73	leader	149
keen	7	label	121	leaf	38
keep	110	labor	91	learn	38
ketchup	60	ladder	134	leave	68
key	137	lady	26	lecture	15
kick	50	lake	128	left	80
kid	108	lamp	11	leg	8
kidney	94	language	89	legal	141

PHRASE INDEX

PHRASE	VISION	PHRASE	VISION	PHRASE	VISION
legend	25	link	22	loyal	109
leisure	146	lion	111	lucky	148
lemon	152	liquid	24	luggage	56
lend	86	list	89	lumber	133
length	98	little	30	lunar	64
lens	119	live	1	lunch	16
leopard	17	lizard	109	luxury	34
lesson	116	load	34	lyrics	129
letter	140	loan	123	machine	100
level	84	lobster	121	mad	56
liar	54	local	135	magic	53
liberty	56	lock	34	magnet	23
library	97	logic	78	maid	152
license	151	lonely	149	mail	92
life	1	long	89	main	107
lift	71	loop	110	major	52
light	43	lottery	25	make	135
like	13	loud	33	mammal	107
limb	31	lounge	57	man	32
limit	25	love	63	manage	151

PHRASE INDEX

PHRASE	VISION	PHRASE	VISION	PHRASE	VISION
mandate	41	maze	137	metal	109
mango	22	meadow	111	method	78
mansion	77	mean	24	middle	116
manual	22	measure	89	midnight	118
maple	137	meat	30	milk	57
marble	85	mechanic	1	million	128
march	100	medal	109	mimic	96
margin	23	media	34	mind	4
marine	27	melody	123	minimum	27
market	84	melt	121	minor	24
marriage	91	member	135	minute	27
mask	101	memory	34	miracle	143
mass	48	mention	78	mirror	129
master	39	menu	149	misery	24
match	67	mercy	89	miss	105
material	151	merge	110	mistake	37
math	130	merit	25	mix	6
matrix	135	merry	33	mixed	145
matter	79	mesh	57	mixture	120
maximum	155	message	63	mobile	35

PHRASE INDEX

PHRASE	VISION	PHRASE	VISION	PHRASE	VISION
model	63	much	96	near	47
modify	64	muffin	65	neck	63
mom	18	mule	72	need	14
moment	77	multiply	114	negative	96
monitor	30	muscle	105	neglect	105
monkey	59	museum	8	neither	85
monster	14	mushroom	19	nephew	36
month	151	music	42	nerve	27
moon	27	must	47	nest	142
moral	75	mutual	19	net	73
more	9	myself	68	network	10
morning	64	mystery	26	neutral	79
mosquito	48	myth	90	never	113
mother	49	naive	37	news	36
motion	61	name	32	next	131
motor	61	napkin	27	nice	27
mountain	90	narrow	26	night	141
mouse	74	nasty	83	noble	59
move	46	nation	118	noise	45
movie	149	nature	77	nominee	56

PHRASE INDEX

PHRASE	VISION	PHRASE	VISION	PHRASE	VISION
noodle	134	obtain	106	only	2
normal	47	obvious	101	open	27
north	131	occur	91	opera	81
nose	144	ocean	38	opinion	152
notable	54	october	133	oppose	147
note	109	odor	43	option	125
nothing	32	off	146	orange	146
notice	102	offer	89	orbit	134
novel	42	office	42	orchard	44
now	33	often	19	order	96
nuclear	39	oil	30	ordinary	142
number	49	okay	80	organ	121
nurse	120	old	138	orient	66
nut	31	olive	55	original	66
oak	93	olympic	128	orphan	42
obey	3	omit	58	ostrich	98
object	153	once	33	other	91
oblige	131	one	132	outdoor	93
obscure	112	onion	60	outer	119
observe	26	online	53	output	125

PHRASE INDEX

PHRASE	VISION	PHRASE	VISION	PHRASE	VISION
outside	41	parade	39	penalty	62
oval	121	parent	121	pencil	10
oven	127	park	13	people	137
over	46	parrot	52	pepper	69
own	33	party	91	perfect	1
owner	40	pass	69	permit	118
oxygen	88	patch	11	person	63
oyster	55	path	49	pet	105
ozone	97	patient	71	phone	80
pact	49	patrol	137	photo	97
paddle	126	pattern	34	phrase	68
page	42	pause	145	physical	122
pair	33	pave	134	piano	4
palace	129	payment	141	picnic	58
palm	152	peace	85	picture	83
panda	29	peanut	98	piece	37
panel	30	pear	107	pig	45
panic	72	peasant	16	pigeon	130
panther	141	pelican	128	pill	103
paper	108	pen	25	pilot	65

PHRASE INDEX

PHRASE	VISION	PHRASE	VISION	PHRASE	VISION
pink	7	pole	122	present	29
pioneer	9	police	155	pretty	118
pipe	81	pond	78	prevent	67
pistol	143	pony	77	price	107
pitch	16	pool	57	pride	3
pizza	24	popular	10	primary	35
place	91	portion	151	print	49
planet	9	position	38	priority	34
plastic	60	possible	117	prison	46
plate	86	post	68	private	109
play	26	potato	121	prize	6
please	129	pottery	133	problem	48
pledge	125	poverty	81	process	42
pluck	6	powder	69	produce	39
plug	150	power	87	profit	111
plunge	40	practice	7	program	7
poem	10	praise	108	project	64
poet	10	predict	1	promote	17
point	107	prefer	153	proof	3
polar	51	prepare	155	property	145

221

PHRASE INDEX

PHRASE	VISION	PHRASE	VISION	PHRASE	VISION
prosper	139	pyramid	116	ranch	19
protect	59	quality	70	random	11
proud	32	quantum	27	range	69
provide	59	quarter	144	rapid	99
public	103	question	59	rare	150
pudding	111	quick	71	rate	33
pull	18	quit	92	rather	70
pulp	122	quiz	144	raven	130
pulse	73	quote	150	raw	46
pumpkin	141	rabbit	79	razor	130
punch	16	raccoon	64	ready	16
pupil	43	race	31	real	107
puppy	124	rack	78	reason	146
purchase	156	radar	140	rebel	7
purity	5	radio	58	rebuild	51
purpose	58	rail	76	recall	140
purse	82	rain	61	receive	7
push	113	raise	36	recipe	33
put	113	rally	7	record	40
puzzle	34	ramp	153	recycle	142

PHRASE	VISION	PHRASE	VISION	PHRASE	VISION
reduce	34	repair	34	ribbon	65
reflect	13	repeat	139	rice	8
reform	42	replace	25	rich	78
refuse	38	report	49	ride	34
region	12	require	50	ridge	138
regret	70	rescue	135	rifle	41
regular	149	resemble	118	right	30
reject	13	resist	1	rigid	47
relax	151	resource	70	ring	11
release	130	response	7	riot	69
relief	43	result	18	ripple	52
rely	109	retire	92	risk	50
remain	9	retreat	143	ritual	141
remember	28	return	88	rival	34
remind	14	reunion	112	river	50
remove	88	reveal	80	road	85
render	86	review	98	roast	37
renew	86	reward	23	robot	3
rent	40	rhythm	139	robust	128
reopen	156	rib	91	rocket	57

PHRASE INDEX

PHRASE	VISION	PHRASE	VISION	PHRASE	VISION
romance	35	safe	28	scene	108
roof	61	sail	87	scheme	135
rookie	83	salad	48	school	143
room	50	salmon	122	science	93
rose	36	salon	6	scissors	157
rotate	81	salt	130	scorpion	69
rough	2	salute	121	scout	14
round	80	same	80	scrap	115
route	155	sample	119	screen	144
royal	131	sand	31	script	113
rubber	121	satisfy	142	scrub	81
rude	26	satoshi	123	sea	67
rug	3	sauce	63	search	98
rule	71	sausage	35	season	37
run	40	save	132	seat	28
runway	20	say	51	second	83
rural	98	scale	76	secret	2
sad	148	scan	86	section	68
saddle	125	scare	102	security	5
sadness	50	scatter	61	seed	18

PHRASE INDEX

PHRASE	VISION	PHRASE	VISION	PHRASE	VISION
seek	77	sheriff	59	siege	93
segment	14	shield	12	sight	59
select	90	shift	18	sign	21
sell	17	shine	31	silent	111
seminar	121	ship	147	silk	14
senior	66	shiver	69	silly	77
sense	120	shock	17	silver	27
sentence	14	shoe	12	similar	55
series	143	shoot	96	simple	11
service	115	shop	32	since	153
session	155	short	149	sing	73
settle	43	shoulder	135	siren	54
setup	74	shove	125	sister	75
seven	33	shrimp	56	situate	5
shadow	76	shrug	27	six	94
shaft	59	shuffle	2	size	89
shallow	43	shy	41	skate	102
share	150	sibling	131	sketch	2
shed	144	sick	21	ski	63
shell	7	side	143	skill	38

PHRASE INDEX

PHRASE	VISION	PHRASE	VISION	PHRASE	VISION
skin	68	snack	67	sort	12
skirt	155	snake	76	soul	143
skull	89	snap	126	sound	114
slab	144	sniff	67	soup	123
slam	146	snow	140	source	104
sleep	103	soap	37	south	61
slender	138	soccer	99	space	50
slice	140	social	41	spare	141
slide	141	sock	83	spatial	110
slight	125	soda	18	spawn	72
slim	141	soft	145	speak	126
slogan	104	solar	138	special	150
slot	9	soldier	130	speed	33
slow	44	solid	155	spell	152
slush	66	solution	80	spend	61
small	11	solve	100	sphere	15
smart	73	someone	104	spice	69
smile	76	song	37	spider	44
smoke	25	soon	40	spike	128
smooth	83	sorry	46	spin	5

PHRASE INDEX

PHRASE	VISION	PHRASE	VISION	PHRASE	VISION
spirit	131	stand	157	strike	71
split	81	start	9	strong	40
spoil	123	state	68	struggle	30
sponsor	101	stay	126	student	128
spoon	72	steak	86	stuff	80
sport	56	steel	58	stumble	13
spot	155	stem	131	style	114
spray	147	step	97	subject	134
spread	118	stereo	8	submit	6
spring	28	stick	60	subway	145
spy	136	still	66	success	10
square	59	sting	98	such	58
squeeze	87	stock	66	sudden	35
squirrel	41	stomach	126	suffer	34
stable	72	stone	52	sugar	144
stadium	10	stool	92	suggest	85
staff	54	story	132	suit	40
stage	9	stove	110	summer	103
stairs	68	strategy	99	sun	41
stamp	66	street	50	sunny	130

PHRASE INDEX

PHRASE	VISION	PHRASE	VISION	PHRASE	VISION
sunset	127	swing	35	teach	15
super	80	switch	79	team	39
supply	104	sword	112	tell	31
supreme	53	symbol	66	ten	102
sure	63	symptom	73	tenant	93
surface	101	syrup	129	tennis	84
surge	156	system	7	tent	34
surprise	17	table	156	term	76
surround	89	tackle	9	test	49
survey	21	tag	129	text	132
suspect	96	tail	17	thank	2
sustain	71	talent	94	that	40
swallow	26	talk	112	theme	143
swamp	142	tank	35	then	101
swap	105	tape	135	theory	81
swarm	62	target	27	there	113
swear	51	task	79	they	133
sweet	4	taste	148	thing	134
swift	61	tattoo	76	this	120
swim	96	taxi	17	thought	156

PHRASE INDEX

PHRASE	VISION	PHRASE	VISION	PHRASE	VISION
three	123	toe	26	toward	53
thrive	85	together	139	tower	49
throw	122	toilet	95	town	82
thumb	137	token	13	toy	144
thunder	94	tomato	47	track	99
ticket	129	tomorrow	130	trade	125
tide	73	tone	45	traffic	84
tiger	94	tongue	126	tragic	53
tilt	151	tonight	122	train	45
timber	100	tool	75	transfer	44
time	30	tooth	102	trap	98
tiny	113	top	122	trash	45
tip	17	topic	138	travel	115
tired	2	topple	5	tray	112
tissue	98	torch	100	treat	125
title	116	tornado	65	tree	98
toast	132	tortoise	90	trend	32
tobacco	66	toss	29	trial	63
today	55	total	144	tribe	36
toddler	84	tourist	32	trick	61

PHRASE INDEX

PHRASE	VISION	PHRASE	VISION	PHRASE	VISION
trigger	74	twelve	138	unique	92
trim	43	twenty	42	unit	57
trip	36	twice	80	universe	69
trophy	48	twin	35	unknown	4
trouble	12	twist	28	unlock	40
truck	147	two	53	until	73
true	33	type	83	unusual	105
truly	96	typical	120	unveil	140
trumpet	29	ugly	70	update	74
trust	103	umbrella	45	upgrade	4
truth	113	unable	95	uphold	140
try	12	unaware	115	upon	21
tube	97	uncle	42	upper	25
tuition	35	uncover	81	upset	74
tumble	23	under	35	urban	83
tuna	109	undo	117	urge	54
tunnel	114	unfair	20	usage	18
turkey	133	unfold	129	use	96
turn	82	unhappy	152	used	99
turtle	128	uniform	53	useful	19

PHRASE INDEX

PHRASE	VISION	PHRASE	VISION	PHRASE	VISION
useless	83	verb	119	vital	38
usual	97	verify	57	vivid	12
utility	103	version	43	vocal	136
vacant	64	very	20	voice	102
vacuum	102	vessel	28	void	51
vague	46	veteran	74	volcano	73
valid	108	viable	20	volume	47
valley	101	vibrant	119	vote	146
valve	113	vicious	37	voyage	35
van	92	victory	94	wage	128
vanish	68	video	118	wagon	8
vapor	113	view	130	wait	116
various	81	village	18	walk	112
vast	67	vintage	67	wall	3
vault	14	violin	73	walnut	8
vehicle	37	virtual	52	want	17
velvet	133	virus	30	warfare	31
vendor	39	visa	89	warm	23
venture	93	visit	29	warrior	65
venue	15	visual	40	wash	54

PHRASE INDEX

PHRASE	VISION	PHRASE	VISION	PHRASE	VISION
wasp	41	wheel	68	wish	95
waste	147	when	119	witness	24
water	150	where	1	wolf	23
wave	54	whip	60	woman	38
way	87	whisper	147	wonder	105
wealth	87	wide	52	wood	55
weapon	8	width	24	wool	59
wear	145	wife	145	word	113
weasel	88	wild	28	work	89
weather	132	will	41	world	106
web	153	win	93	worry	33
wedding	66	window	82	worth	62
weekend	130	wine	124	wrap	155
weird	19	wing	43	wreck	7
welcome	149	wink	68	wrestle	107
west	77	winner	117	wrist	30
wet	145	winter	117	write	118
whale	39	wire	28	wrong	18
what	116	wisdom	15	yard	21
wheat	106	wise	139	year	127

PHRASE INDEX

PHRASE	VISION	PHRASE	VISION	PHRASE	VISION
yellow	141	youth	98	zone	1
you	156	zebra	88	zoo	34
young	29	zero	110		

www.ingramcontent.com/pod-product-compliance
Lightning Source LLC
Chambersburg PA
CBHW071241050326
40690CB00011B/2208